REWIRE YOUR BRAIN

RID YOUR MIND OF NEGATIVE THOUGHTS AND LIMITING BELIEFS, STOP OVERTHINKING AND CREATE HEALTHY HABITS.

JACK THOMAS

CONTENTS

INTRODUCTION

HAVE YOU EVER WANTED TO LEARN HOW TO DEAL WITH LIMITING BELIEFS? HOW DO YOU OVERCOME THEM?

First, write down the belief and play detective and follow your thoughts and emotions around. Discover what holds you back and also how strongly you hold each belief. You now need to acknowledge that although these are beliefs you formed about yourself in the past because of circumstances surrounding you, this doesn't make the beliefs true. As real as they feel, you have to either defend the beliefs or achieve your goals and desires. If you argue for your limitations, you get to keep them. But you also get to lose the possibility of succeeding and finally being free to enjoy your desires and the success that comes with achieving your goals.

Using your imagination, believe something different. For example, tell yourself, "I've let so many great opportunities pass, I've learned how to identify when I'm self-sabotaging" or "Now that I've been in an unhappy marriage, I know that happiness comes from within, and my partner's job is not to complete me but complement me and my happiness." Tell yourself this enough times, the same way you told yourself you aren't enough, and you will start believing it. But saying something to yourself is not enough. Instead, go a step further and feel it.

Now, it's time to take action and do something different. You may be scared out of your mind, but start acting as a true embodiment of who you want to be. If you are the best at your job, how do you act when working on projects? What feelings do you have, and what do you tell yourself about the project and yourself? If you had the best marriage ever, how would you act around your partner? If you are the kind of person who lives an alternative green life, where would you shop, and what items would you pick? Not taking action on your new beliefs only reenforces the old beliefs. So, this step is critical to your growth.

Emotions play an essential role in how you think and behave. Each emotion you feel compels you to take action and influences the decisions you make in your life, whether the decisions are large or small. To understand how these two are related, let's first understand the components of an emotion.

First, there is the subject component, which refers to how you experience an emotion. Second, we have the physical part, which is how your body reacts to the emotions, and lastly, the expressive component or how you behave in response to the emotion.

HOW TO BETTER CHANGE YOUR BELIEF SYSTEM AND YOUR SUBCONSCIOUS MIND

You will learn how to change your belief system literally, to reprogram your subconscious mind for happiness. You must be aware of it before you can alter it. Start with the idea that your subconscious mind can become conscious.

You believe you are responsible for what you do, say, and think, but it's not really like that. That's how you want it to be. The fact is that you use an autopilot most of the time without a lot of awareness of why you do what you do, say what you do, perceive what you feel, and interpret the world in the way you do. How many times did you say to yourself, "How could I have said that? Or done that? What was I thinking?" How many times do you drive on the highway for miles and miles only to realize you don't remember the last five miles?

Have you ever looked at the person with whom you live and realized how much he or she looks like one of your own parents? (Although you didn't know when you met them and fell in love with them.)

When was the last time you tried to change a really bad habit, like smoking or drinking, and gave up in spite of all your good intentions after some false beginnings?

If you observe an inner resistance every time you consider pursuing an idea, learning a skill, or doing anything you truly wish to do, that's because of the fears and limiting beliefs you have created over the years.

Many of us are in the habit of putting ourselves down or lowering our morale by suggesting negative ideas. If you habitually say things like, "I cannot do this," "This is too difficult to learn," "I can never become successful," "This is not my color," "I am scared of failing," or similar things, this explains why your go-to thought for every-thing is a negative one.

Years of negative self-talk create an inner critic inside you, a pesky, strong voice that always spews venom inside your mind. This voice gives rise to your fears, toxic beliefs, and limiting ideas that keep you from moving forward in life.

Every time you say things such as, "My life is terri-ble," your subconscious mind writes down "terrible life" in your inner code; this then shapes your attitude toward your life.

That is why you feel scared of taking risks. It's also why you don't believe in yourself, give in to your tempta-tions, quit your goals midway, have low self-esteem, and don't live your life the way you want to. The right way to change that is to calm your inner critic and then gently replace it with a supportive inner voice, in order to build a positive and growth-oriented mindset.

Here Are Strategies to Help You Do That:

Pay Attention to and Acknowledge Your Inner Critic

First, you need to learn to be aware of your negative inner voice so that you can understand what it says, acknowledge it, and then consciously replace it with positive suggestions. Shunning that voice without listening to it only gives it the power to grow stronger inside you.

Here's what you should do:

- Every time you observe some sort of agitation inside you when you think of pursuing an idea, sit somewhere alone for a while and pay attention to the different thoughts orbiting your mind.
- Pick one thought at a time, and before you analyze it, be grateful to your subconscious mind for highlighting this concern. If you thought, "I will fail my exam," the first thing you should do is acknowledge this concern without letting yourself become emotional and irrational about it.
- Next, assess and scrutinize that concern very objectively and patiently. Instead of perceiving it as a negative thought, think of it as a concern. When you shift your perspective toward it, it stops overwhelming or scaring you.
- Assess the genuineness of the thought and

see if there is any proof to validate it. If you feel you will fail your exam, what reason do you have to believe that? If you have failed exams before, which is why you feel doomed for failure this time around too, understand that the past is the past, and you cannot go back in time.

- Continue having a discussion with your inner critic by genuinely describing and justifying your viewpoint.

Work on these steps every time a debilitating thought disturbs you. Once your inner critic calms down a little, feed positive suggestions to your subconscious mind.

Replace Negative Thoughts With Positive Ones

The instant your inner critic silences a little, use that opportunity to replace that negative thought with a more realistically positive one. For instance, if earlier you thought, "I cannot lose weight," change it to, "I can lose weight. I am managing my weight well by eating healthy foods and exercising daily."

Ensure to suggest that you are already working on your goal because this way, your subconscious will accept it and encourage you to take meaningful action toward your goal in the present moment.

As shown in the suggestion above, suggest how you are achieving your goal. This way, you will understand the actions you need to take to fulfill a goal and start working on them.

Chant the Positive Thought Repeatedly

Once you have a positive substitute for a particular negative thought, chant it repeatedly. Remember that your subconscious accepts suggestions it feels are important to you. It judges this by looking at how frequently you focus on and recall something. The more you chant a suggestion, the better your subconscious focuses on it.

This aspect of your subconscious is under the control of the Reticular Activating System (RAS) in your brain. This system filters unnecessary information from the important pieces and shifts your attention towards the important information.

When you chant a suggestion repeatedly, it activates the RAS, and you will be able to focus better on that idea. It stays in your sight, and you remember it regularly. This way, you keep your subconscious engaged in that idea, create more positive thoughts centered on it, and draw great experiences your way to manifest that reality.

Work on Your Fears

As you slowly train yourself to think positively and consciously, replace your negative ideas with uplifting ones. Start working on your fears in the same manner. Try out this method:

- Create a list of all the fears that keep you from achieving your goals.

- Pick any one fear you would like to work on first.
- Find the root cause of that fear, which is likely to be a negative and limiting belief.
- Create positive replacements for that belief and chant them repeatedly; do it daily even.
- Write those positive suggestions on a piece of paper, make copies, and put them up in different parts of your house so that every time you move past that note, you remember the positive beliefs and focus on them better.

If you consistently work on these guidelines, you will soon get rid of all your fears, nurture a positive mindset, and learn how to control your subconscious mind better so that you can make every day of your life more meaningful.

To ensure your subconscious helps you achieve your targets, you need clarity of purpose and a burning desire to accomplish your goals. The next chapter will help you do that.

CHAPTER 1

WHAT DO WE MEAN BY THOUGHTS, VALUES, AND BELIEFS?

A THOUGHT IS something that can appear in your mind rapidly and exit just as fast without leaving any significant effect. You think about it for a second and then move onto something else. However, there are also thoughts that have the potential to affect your mind and trigger a surge of emotion that cannot be suppressed. These thoughts touch your inner feelings. So, where does a thought come from? They originate from the visual information that your eyes perceive, or things your ears hear or your nose smells ... or in short, anything you perceive with your senses.

For example, imagine one fine morning you are out jogging and you notice a pretty girl jogging in the opposite direction. Your mind may transiently think about her sexually, but this thought leaves rapidly. This is just a momentary thought, you have no relationship with the girl, and the thought is simply triggered by your visual perception of her. You continue jogging and you notice a single car passing by slowly; you look at it momentarily and come to the realization that you do not know where the car is going, nor where it has come from. This thought is once again triggered by a momentary visual perception; it was not attached to enhanced emotion or feeling, it was just a thought and not thinking; therefore, your mind was in a state of nonthinking.

THE PLACE WHERE THINKING STARTS AND ENDS

Now, if it were that simple, things would be much different. For example, if the girl that you spotted jogging resembled your ex in any way, your thought may come with attached emotion, and you may plummet into a spiral of thinking. You will be overwhelmed by emotion, and you will begin to ask yourself, "What is it about her that makes me think of my ex?" This is an example of casual thoughts developing into thinking within your mind. This may trigger a relay of thoughts about your ex as you begin to wonder what she's doing now and who she is with. As you jog past a café, you realize that this café was the location of your first date, and these thoughts about her keep coming, like a conveyor belt. A stream of thoughts is initiated within your mind; this is thinking, and it only subsides when your attention drifts away.

In a similar way, if you witness a car passing you by and notice that the woman in the passenger seat resembles your wife, you may be startled and your emotional state may be ruffled. You may begin to have thoughts about your wife cheating on you and convince yourself that the person driving the car was her lover. What is the reason behind this? If the relationship you have with your wife is not the best, she could hide anything from you, regardless of whether she is having an affair or not. This will evoke feelings of sadness and suspicion; these are the sort of thoughts that upset you and tend to drive you mad. These thoughts continue oscillating in your mind as the flow of these negative thoughts increases. These thoughts will not stop until you either uncover the truth or avoid finding the truth. Through this, a simple thought has spiraled into excessive thinking.

Therefore, a thought may instantly disappear from your mind just as quickly as it appeared. However, these loaded thoughts that are attached to emotion usually lead to further consecutive thoughts of a similar nature. This is thinking, and it is a continuous flow of successive thoughts.

Your thoughts will be there at every step of the way in your life, and if you don't do anything about them, they will control it all. This is a cycle that is there to help you, and it will if all conditions are favorable. But, sometimes, they're not. Sometimes, being upset or angry at one thing can cause you to lash out in other ways just because you were already in that mood. Your perception of events around you can be influenced just because you've seen that they will be related to the feelings that you have. Your mindset matters in every aspect.

The fact that thoughts, feelings, and behaviors all cycle together is both a blessing and a curse at the same time. You know that you are able to control them because of the way that they function. Yes, they may be out of your control, but think about the one thing in this world that you can control: yourself. You can make choices for yourself. You can choose different actions or behaviors. You can choose to believe in certain things. While emotions themselves are instantaneous and difficult to alter, you can learn to harness them by knowing that you can change the thoughts behind them.

WHAT IS THINKING?

Thinking is the mental activity that moves us from doubt towards certainty. There are two types of thoughts: those that we are aware of and those that we are not. The truth is, we often don't pay any attention to the inner workings of our minds despite just how powerful they can be. Think back to the last time you were frustrated or angry at someone that you love. It could be your spouse, your child, your best friend, your parents, or anyone else. Think of the last time that you snapped at them and said something that you didn't mean. You might have quickly apologized for it, but did you ever stop to think about why you said what you said in the first place? What drove you to such frustrated thoughts? Why did you snap or lash out? What did you have to gain by doing so?

Chances are, even if you can't identify it yet, the reason that you did so had nothing to do with the outburst in the first place. In fact, there is a good chance that the outburst that you had was actually a symptom of a bigger problem. That problem is probably some sort of negative thought that you had lurking somewhere in your mind. You may not even be aware of what that thought is. It can be daunting to think that something that you might not even be able to identify or become aware of is actually able to control you. But this is exactly the case—you are the sum of your thoughts. Your thoughts control everything. Your thoughts will weigh you down. They will prevent you from finding success in life. They will hold you back and make you feel like you have no choice but to give in to them.

Though your thoughts have significant power over you, if you don't know what you're doing, you can actually tame them. You can learn to control them so that you can better your own situation. You can learn to control your thoughts and change your own brain. Do you tend to behave negatively? You can teach yourself to stop. The brain is incredibly plastic and is always learning, whether we want it to or not, and that is exactly how those negative thoughts can control you if you don't know what you are doing.

BELIEF

Belief is the energy behind the placebo effect. However, this psychological power isn't seen just in remarkable placebo studies and infrequent cases of spontaneous recovery. Your beliefs operate for or against you daily in each area of your life.

Think about beliefs as psychological applications installed in your mind that take in raw information through your perceptions and apply significance to it. If you see that, "My weight has not changed this week," you might think, "This implies that this diet does not work and I will never get rid of the weight."

You generated beliefs regarding what you believed your results implied, but your thoughts might have been wrong. Your nutrition program might be quite effective, but you may have underestimated just how much you're eating. You may have gained water weight or increased fresh muscle tissue, decreasing weight reduction.

You have beliefs about your surroundings, your behaviors, your abilities, as well as your own identity. As soon as you develop a belief, you are going to act like it is true, and you're going to withstand often or filter out anything that disagrees with it. When it comes to nutrition and diet, a lot of men and women believe in things with an almost religious certainty. Low-carb diets, for example, have valid fat-loss advantages like decreasing appetite and controlling insulin.

Unfortunately, whenever someone is effective with a low-carb diet, they frequently take on dogmatic and erroneous beliefs. They may look at virtually all carbs as fattening, or they may frequently feel that calories do not count, a harmful and false belief. But try convincing a previously obese low-carb dieter of this (it is about as simple as getting them to change their faith).

Incidentally, if you are a successful high-carb/low-fat dieter, do not gloat too much, since confused beliefs about high-carb/low-fat diets are just as common. Some beliefs are a lot more powerful than others. With the potential exception of religious beliefs, individuality beliefs are the most powerful of all. It's possible to spot a belief in your individuality by what you say after "I'm." "I'm an overeater" is an identity notion.

Beliefs should be respected and honored, but they must also be inspected carefully. A belief is just a generalization. If you take the risk that you may be thinking things which are really holding you back, then you have taken the first step toward altering your behavior, your entire body, and your own life.

All of us know that a belief is confidence or trust in something. But most of us do not realize that beliefs are not necessarily based on a rational ground. Most of our core beliefs are developed during our childhood and are not supported by logical proofs. They stay in our subconscious and guide our perception and behavior without us knowing it. Our childhood irrational beliefs control most of our behavior even today. Sounds funny?

Our belief system is a cohesive set of mutually dependent beliefs. One belief supports the viability of the other, and it proceeds as a chain of beliefs and resulting thoughts and ideas. You can also visualize the belief system as a hierarchical set of beliefs where basic beliefs act as the roots and the dependent thoughts as the child nodes.

Our core beliefs are self-explanatory and primitive in nature. These beliefs stand strong without the support of other beliefs.

Our belief system acts as a filter through which we process our experience and perceive the outer world. It is through this filter that we act upon our surroundings in return. In simple words, it is due to our beliefs that the things, situations, experiences make sense to us, and it is our beliefs that govern the way we behave. We are what we believe ourselves to be (so true is this statement).

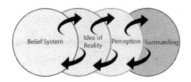

LIMITING BELIEFS

These are deep-rooted beliefs that force us to live a life that lacks fulfillment. Decisions made under the influence of these beliefs do not allow individuals to become the best version of themselves.

From our early childhood on, we receive many negative messages that we internalize as adults. These messages, when coped with badly, result in self-sabotage during adulthood.

Sometimes blatantly harmful results occur, e.g., constantly getting in trouble with the law because you internalized the message you heard growing up, "You will never amount to anything." Other times subtle but destructive nonetheless results happen, e.g., never taking the SATs because of the belief "No one in my family made it past high school. I surely won't go to college." Limiting beliefs are at the core of criminality and despair.

Limiting beliefs come in all shapes and sizes. Some

are as destructive as the thoughts in the examples, others are waiting for the right time to become equally as bad. In either case, the results generally ensure that one does not live up to their full potential.

As children, we have grand visions for the future. Limiting beliefs are what guarantee that the same dream and visions for us as adults are nothing but infantile megalomania.

This is because as we age, we start relying too much on our ego. As a result, we worry about looking good in other people's eyes, and we fear falling off our perceived social status. We try to fit in, to conform to mainstream culture. We try to conform to the norms of society, and we forget that we once had a dream for ourselves.

We disassociate ourselves from that dream because we fear being labeled a "pariah," chasing after it. So, we reject the possibility of greatness, fearing the potential of isolation.

We see examples of people that are larger than life on a daily basis, people such as Oprah Winfrey, Bill Gates, Dalai Lama, Nelson Mandela, Warren Buffet, and Steve Jobs. However, no sooner are we done reading about or watching a documentary on them, we convince ourselves that such feats are impossible for us.

We put greatness on a pedestal and look in awe at the contributions made to the world by others, silently dismissing the possibility of ourselves adding massive value to others and being recognized for it.

We blame this on a cornucopia of external reasons.

Rarely does the list of excuses contain the real reason, our own limiting beliefs.

Limiting beliefs are also statements that we tell ourselves that convince us that there are disaster and peril on the other side of risk.

Limiting beliefs are the reason we will never be able to give freely to the world the gift that we are meant to give.

Example:

Sarah, a painter by choice, is extremely passionate about painting but watches opportunities pass her by because she doesn't think her art is good enough for a large show.

She is resentful of those who get their paintings displayed at galas in front of a large and diverse audience.

In actuality, it takes a lot of effort even for great artists to be showcased at high profile fundraisers. Sarah, owing to her perfectionistic attitude, always feared rejection and is never persistent in her actions to be showcased at such events.

Her limiting belief of "My painting is not good enough for galas" holds her back from the effort required to be showcased at prominent venues.

THE CONSCIOUS MIND

It is important to understand the features of the "conscious" mind before we can fully grasp the influence of the subconscious mind. The conscious mind of man is a formidable and magnificent development. The simplest definition of your conscious mind is that it's the part you're aware of in your head. It regulates your thoughts and works on your own will. The conscious mind is the mind's logical component too. It's the part of the mind that has the power to objectively think about a situation, evaluate it, and make a factor-based decision. Likewise, as you analyze and learn from previous errors, that's your conscious mind at work. That's another example of the conscious mind at work as you go through the process of setting goals for the future. Often you might hear someone say, "I made a conscious decision to do that." That is the conscious mind's strength.

But as great as the conscious mind is, it has intrinsic limits, too. For one thing, there's minimal memory in the conscious mind. How much trouble do you have remembering someone's name or even remembering where your keys are? Those are examples of the conscious mind's restricted memory. Another weakness of the conscious mind is that it can only do one thing at a time. If it attempts to do more than one thing at a time, it will turn back and forth very quickly. One example might be reading when someone is talking to you. Your conscious mind can concentrate on what you're reading at any given moment, or it can concentrate on listening to what you're being told. But at the same time, it cannot dwell on both. As the word "aware" means, at any given moment the conscious mind cannot do something on which it is not "consciously" centered. And it is here where the subconscious mind comes into action.

THE SUBCONSCIOUS MIND

Whereas the conscious mind is that portion of your mind that you are aware of, the subconscious mind is considered the portion of your mind that you are not aware of. The subconscious mind is on duty 24 hours a day, and at the same time it can perform an infinite number of functions. It is like a machine running in your brain that continuously monitors your unconscious actions, emotions, and behaviors. If you're wide awake or deep asleep, your subconscious mind is actively at work manipulating all of your body's vital functions, with no help from your conscious mind. You don't have to think constantly about breathing, making your heart pound, digesting your food, blinking your eyes, and so on. Your subconscious mind, whether you are asleep or awake, does all that for you around the clock. The subconscious mind interacts continuously with every cell in your body, receives feedback from those cells, and sends instructions to them. The subconscious mind also manages all the repetitive things you had to learn in your conscious mind through a lengthy process. The challenge of learning to drive a car is a classic example. When you first learned to drive a car, think back to that. You had to think carefully at first about all that you did. So, as you go through the active learning cycle, neuropathways will be established in the brain, and your subconscious mind takes slowly over, so you don't have to think about every movement or action consciously.

The same method applies to any of the things you've

learned to do consciously ... riding a bike, tying up your shoes, swimming, you name it. These are all examples of things you had to learn to do consciously, through a tedious process, but after you went through the conscious process, the subconscious mind took over, and now you can do certain things without thinking about them consciously.

CHAPTER 2

THE CONSCIOUS MIND

THE FOREMOST BASIC description of your conscious mind is that it's the part of your mind you're conscious of. Your conscious mind (the part that you are aware of) is responsible for identifying various information through the use of the five senses—sight, smell, taste, touch, and hearing—and making decisions based on what is relevant in your life. Subsequently, the decisions that you make with your conscious mind affect your subconscious. You may have heard it many times that the influence of the subconscious mind in one person's behavior is 88%, while the conscious mind influences the remaining 12%. But the newest research has proven that the subconscious mind is responsible for 95% to 99%, and determines almost all decisions, actions, emotions, and behaviors of one person. In other words, the subconscious mind is 99 times more powerful than the conscious mind.

When there is a conflict between the conscious and the subconscious mind, the subconscious mind will win.

When there is a conflict between thoughts and emotions, emotions will win. One thing you need to note is don't force yourself to think positively, especially when you are feeling negative! Many books always advise you to think positively when you feel negative. For example, you set a goal, but you feel uncomfortable and negative self-talk appears, "I can't achieve it." Most books advise you to change the negative self-talk into positive thoughts, "No! It is not true! I can achieve it! Believe in yourself! Yes, I can achieve it!" Well, don't ever do this! Because this is an act of self-destruction.

Human memories are holographic, so they have an ability to cross-reference. There is no stand-alone memory. I believe you have often experienced this. Have you ever thought something and ended up thinking something else? Maybe you thought of your income, and then you thought about your company, then the traffic jam, then a car, then your cousin, and so on. From one thought to another thought. One memory is associated with another memory. Everything is interrelated.

The same thing happens when you feel negative and try to think positively. Do you know that it will trigger negative memories in the subconscious mind? In this context, the more you try to be positive, the more negative you become. This is rarely recognized and understood by most people. I have often met people who become stressed because of positive thinking.

When you feel negative and try to think positively, you actually suppress your negative emotion. The negative emotions don't go anywhere, they are still in your subconscious mind. If you let them reside in there too long, it will become an illness, stress, and in the worst cases, suicide.

When you feel negative, positive thinking is only worsening your condition. To get the benefits of positive thinking, you first need to feel positive!

Your thoughts are in charge of your behaviors. But if your emotions rule or dominate you, emotions will beat thoughts and take over your behaviors. When you are ruled by your emotions, it is hard to think rationally, and that's when your emotion takes over your behavior. Your emotion takes over your behavior, and you will behave according to your emotion.

The most obvious example is a phobia. If you have a phobia, when you see or feel what you fear, you will end up being afraid without being able to analyze whether it is scary or not. When the fear dominates you, you will behave according to it; you will run, scream, or faint.

So, where does emotion come from? An emotion appears or is triggered because of a certain stimulus. When you get a certain stimulus, the stimulus will then activate a certain memory in your subconscious mind, and the memory will then bring a certain emotion. For example, a song. When you hear a certain song, it makes you remember a certain moment in your life, and it will make you feel happy, sad, excited, etc.

A stimulus will also activate your belief system. Beliefs are what you believe to be true. A belief system is a set of or a group of beliefs that create a system and influence how you think, feel, and behave. What if you think, feel, and behave in a certain way? Obviously, you will achieve a certain result. But what if the result is not what you want? Then you have to change your belief. But changing belief at the conscious level is not enough, you have to change your belief in the subconscious mind! Change your subconscious belief, change your life!

It gives us the power to think about things, evaluate the facts, analyze the risks, and determine what we believe is the best course of action. It also gives us the power to place together a thoughtful decision to implement the course of action we've decided upon. But as marvelous as the conscious mind is, it also has some inherent limitations. Remember, the conscious mind features a limited memory, and it can do just one thing at a time.

The conscious mind is limited by perception and experience. It works on a garbage in, garbage out principle. It's only as good as its input. We are very limited people because we are products of our specific circumstances. We are only responsible for what we know. This is still a constraint. It would be great if all of us could overcome our conditions and live up to the highest standards, but we're only human.

Another limitation is that we are products of our culture. It's very easy to define culture as involving a certain type of dress and a certain cuisine. Those are shallower cultural differences. Cultural differences actually run much deeper. They influence how you view life, your general attitude, how you get along with others, and how you define the good life. Your culture also plays a big role in what your personal urges and values are.

CONSCIOUS AND UNCONSCIOUS MIND

Did you know that the conscious mind and unconscious mind are in continuous dialogue with each other? There is a border that we all cross daily. And we go through it mostly without becoming aware of what is happening. In the evening, when we fall asleep, and in the morning when we wake up, we cross a threshold, a threshold that separates two worlds. But who tells you that you are sleeping when you lose consciousness? If reality is nothing but the interpretation that the brain makes of the electrical impulses it receives from the five senses, when we sleep, what happens? Read on to find out.

WHEN YOU CHANGE THE WAY YOU SEE THINGS, THINGS YOU SEE CHANGE

The unconscious mind guides your life and everything you rationally think you are doing. In reality, it has been silently suggested to you by that part of you that seems not to be there, that part of you that listens to everything and responds to everything.

The automatic emotional responses that often surface in us in certain situations are information recorded on an unconscious level. When the unconscious mind realizes that it is experiencing a situation it already knows, it offers you the emotional/rational response that it had previously considered most suitable at that moment.

Let me explain: do you know how your browser works to access the internet? While browsing the web, the browser records data and preferences so that when you return to browsing, it will be easier for it to guarantee the most suitable solutions for the type of search you usually do. Here, the unconscious mind works the same way. It registers and reproposes the most suitable solutions for you and does all this to safeguard you and guarantee the best possible experience. But often this information is incorrect, harmful, obsolete, and no longer appropriate at the moment we are living. What do you say, maybe we should update the system every now and then? Or if you prefer, perhaps it is appropriate to change the model and recondition the thought!?

If twenty years ago you were embarrassed in front of the girl you liked, now it will not make sense to chance that embarrassment again. But the unconscious, having not received other information in the duration, will almost certainly propose the same logical/emotional product to you if you ever meet her again. Defusing this automatic reaction is possible by self-suggestion with new thoughts/emotions about the event, obviously before you happen to meet it again.

The unconscious mind is always attentive and susceptible to everything that happens, continuously records your life experience, and records it with greater intensity when what you live or think is wrapped in emotions. The stronger the emotion you feel, the more importance (and priority) your unconscious mind will record.

But returning to what was said earlier, there are two points in time where we cross the threshold of the two worlds that belong to us: when we wake up and when we fall asleep. In these two moments, our life experience and our perception of reality change. We go out of one world to enter another. These two worlds have been chasing each other since we were born, and since we were born, we do nothing but go in and out. You thought you had one life, right? And instead you have two.

And if during the day the rational mind allows us to move in the physical reality that is presented to us, during the night, during the deep sleep phase, it is the unconscious mind that takes the reins of our dream life. The rational mind is silent and observes the spectacle that the unconscious has to offer. The same thing happens when we meditate or when we allow ourselves the luxury of living without logical/rational interference; that is when we contemplate the spectacle of life in the absence of judgment or when we allow ourselves the pleasure of flowing with what we are experiencing.

But it is only in the few moments before crossing the threshold of the two worlds that magic can happen. Here, miracles are literally sown. Have you ever fallen asleep with the thought of something to solve and the following day you found yourself with the solution in your head, as if it had appeared out of nowhere, like a bolt of lightning? Your every request is an order that is always taken in charge and fulfilled. You can call it God, the unconscious, soul, power of the mind, call it what you like, but this characteristic distinguishes you from the other souls of this planet. You are in the act of creating yourself at all times, and those five minutes before bed are of fundamental importance for shaping the reality that you want to experience.

CHAPTER 3

THE BIGGEST MIND YOU DON'T NOTICE

THE SUBCONSCIOUS MIND

THE SUBCONSCIOUS MIND often obeys our directives. How do I mean? This implies whatever command you give to it is what you receive in return. There will be a lot of trouble if it is not programmed in our favor, and we can gain the benefits if we get the correct commands. It will of course receive inputs and discover what is stimulated by our emotions. The subconscious mind is a good messenger but a terrible master. Everything, whether needed or not, is achieved once we have confirmed the related emotions. The greater the intensity of the feelings we receive, the more efficient and promptly we can get goals achieved. How is it processed? A thought, the thought forms an image, an image forms emotion, and the emotion therefore births reality. It could, therefore, mean that we create our thoughts based on whatever it is we've seen, received, or at some point inputted into our mind.

This however implies that we determine or control what comes into our subconscious mind.

So many things have formed the basis of our dispositions due to what has been impressed in us from a very tender age. What we listen to, what we say, and what we think are always a resultant effect of the ideas we have absorbed from our childhood stage. The ideas are what form the reasons behind every decision we take; instead of focusing on solutions and a way out, we tend to attack what is not actually necessary.

When a child steals, some parents, especially in some parts of the world, believe flogging the thief out of the child is the only solution. Even when they are given positive alternatives and measures to help the child, they still resort to serious and severe beating. The big question is: are they interested in the beating of the child or the change? It's so unfortunate that the first decision of punishment comes to our mind rather than the change we indeed want to see. The punishment is now the focus, not the change. As we declare or think of a word, it forms an image in our head, thereby generating stronger emotions in us.

Take, for instance, if I tell you not to imagine a blue orange. What just happened? You picture it right away. It is, however, so important to know that words can go a long way being registered in your mind either negative or positive as the mind does not comprehend negations. Also, if you want to input something into your brain, be focused in imagining the related scene, either in the past or present because it gives you an image of the future.

Let me bring to your attention that as you read this guide, your conscious mind is always engaged because your brain is busy incorporating words seen on the pages by your eyeballs and interpreting them into useful information, but your inner consciousness is certainly at work. It's processing what you have read and has stored a portion of it as a piece of information that will serve as reference in the future through memory. The gathering of this processed information results in the way in which we understand and relate with things in the future.

Work has been tediously done by neuroscientists and psychologists to find rigid and tangible features of the subconscious mind.

The reason why we will wash dishes and suddenly an idea just pops up through our minds is that even when we aren't taking note of this network with consciousness, it is still in our brains.

The field of science isn't too certain on how and why this occurs, but entrepreneurs can affirm the power embedded in subconscious ideas. Of course, there are few strategies that can be put in place to enhance quality functioning of the brain.

We can't determine what happens to us, we can only determine or control how we respond to it. As a matter of fact, it can be argued that the ability or inability of entrepreneurs to respond correctly to the market, for example, will be the sole factor of their success. It is of no doubt that we struggle with our reactions which come to play as emotions, fears, aspirations, and goals. These have the ability to influence how we respond to situations.

Experienced meditators were grouped together to be examined versus people who do not meditate. It was discovered that those who were given to meditation had the special ability of being aware of when their subconscious mind was at work.

More so, in recent times, studies have shown that regular meditation on oneself positively can help us deal easily with fatigue and also improve our skills in getting problems solved. Subconscious beliefs are always more powerful than conscious beliefs, in part because they operate under the surface, and we usually don't know they are there—but they still direct our actions. In fact, if you have two opposing beliefs, one conscious and the other subconscious, the subconscious belief will always dominate.

OWN YOUR SUBCONSCIOUS MIND

Own your subconscious mind, take full ownership of your subconscious mind. It's part of you. It's natural. It's the other half of your consciousness. It is the repository of your unremembered dreams. It is your impulses. It is the great beyond, as far as your mind is concerned. Are you going to constantly run away from this and refuse to tap its unlimited power? Or are you going to own it, warts and all? Taking ownership means refusing to be afraid. There are many things collected by your subconscious mind that you would rather not look at. This may be childhood trauma. This may be sick, twisted, and embarrassing thoughts that you may have. You must overcome your repulsion to these things when you take ownership of your subconscious mind because it is part of you. That fact is they're not going to go away. This is part of you. And if you want to change something or change its direction or make it work towards a better outcome, you must first claim ownership. Stopping fearing taking ownership of your subconscious mind means refusing to feel guilty. If you emotionally beat yourself up regularly, please understand that this is not just some free-floating anxiety. It's not just something that enters your mind because your brain has nothing else better to do. This comes from somewhere. It has a cause. It is not random when you take ownership of your subconscious mind you can start refusing to feel guilty. Feeling guilty is a choice when you feel remorse or regret about certain things that happened in the past or choices that you've made. Those are your interpretations of those facts. You can choose to learn from them and move on. Or you can choose to beat yourself up emotionally over and over again.

It's your choice. Guilt is an emotional interpretation. When you take full ownership of your subconscious, you quickly realize that this is going on. You quickly understand that there are better options out there. Guilt and regrets are powerful as they can hold you back and drag you down. Wouldn't it be better to learn from them and use them the way they were intended? These emotions feel bad because they're intended to teach us. If anything, we're supposed to use them as motivation to make better decisions in the future. When you take ownership, you allow yourself to do this. You allow yourself to be curious again because now you can look at how you've been coping and try to come up with an alternative. If you've been wracked by guilt because you've disappointed your parents for over 30 years, your curiosity might lead to a different interpretation. Or better yet a different coping mechanism. But none of this is going to happen if you continue to stay where you are. If you continue to refuse to take ownership, you will suffer the same results as before.

The bottom line is whatever negative consequences of your actions you're feeling, they arise primarily from your refusal to take ownership of these emotions. Coping mechanisms allow you to choose to cope in different ways. You are not stuck with the way you've done things for years. It may seem like it, but you have a lot more control and a lot more say over your situation than you care to realize. Learn to explore your subconscious mind, start a journal, and explore the things that you fear. Explore how you normally respond to this fear. Please understand that you are looking at circumstantial evidence. In other words, for you to know if the world is round, it's not like you can put yourself in a rocket, shoot yourself thousands of miles up into the atmosphere, and then verify once and for all that the Earth is round. The simpler and more practical way to do it is to wait for the next eclipse. When you see the eclipse, then you know exactly that the Earth's shadow is round. The same applies to your subconscious. There are many ways to explore it, and believe me, a lot of them are very hard. The easiest way to do it is through just circumstantial evidence. Pay close attention to what you are afraid of. You can't quite find a rational reason why you are afraid of certain things. That is your subconscious mind speaking to you. Pay close attention to this list and how it comes out. Come up with a collection of these and then pay attention to the things that you're guilty of or you feel remorseful about. Look at all the negative emotions you have and then pay close attention to them; catalogue them because they start giving you a snapshot of your subconscious mind.

Learn to map out your intuition. Have you ever noticed that in certain situations you tend to say the right things at the right time to produce the right results with the right people? Mostly this is not due to your prior training. A lot of the time this is not because you were groomed to do that kind of thing. Instead, it just came out of you. Well, that is your subconscious mind as well because intuition is a big part of your subconscious mind map that becomes fully aware of that. Wrap your mind around it and take ownership of it. This is not a scary thing. A lot of people think that this is some sort of scene from *The Exorcist* or some horror movie. Judging by how some people talk about this situation, it's as if they're describing that scene in the movie *Alien* where the alien punches a hole through some guy's chest as people were operating on him. Grotesque, sad, and distorted because your subconscious mind is beautiful. Don't be afraid of the beauty of your subconscious mind. Let's get real. A lot of your nightmares come from your subconscious mind because this is the area that you really can't control.

So do a lot of your desires, a lot of your perversions, a lot of your twisted logic, and all that other mental debris you try to segregate unconsciously into your subconscious mind. So, it's kind of like a dumping ground for half-baked, unformed thoughts and frustrated wishes but just like any garbage dump can be located near a beautiful park or a wide-open green field right under a beautiful, wide-open blue endless sky. Your subconscious mind can be a thing of beauty so don't just focus on the things that you'd rather run away from or aren't embarrassed about. Focus on the whole picture. Learn to live in your subconscious mind. Learn to appreciate the things in your subconscious mind and be comfortable in it because this is the key to taking control over it. If there are certain things that you're guilty about, confront them and look at them straight in the eye. Did this happen? And is this a reasonable reaction? You'd be surprised as to how many twisted, painful, tortured memories in your subconscious can be dealt with once and for all when you gather the confidence to stand up to them.

REMOVING BLOCKS AND FEARS TO THE SUBCONSCIOUS MIND

Holding onto negative, self-destructive, and unhelpful thoughts and beliefs stems from a poverty mindset. This is also known as poverty consciousness. For example this may manifest in the belief that it is immoral to desire money and that all rich people are greedy or corrupt. We may also have grown up with the belief that it is hard to become wealthy and that it is an unattainable goal. These sentiments, passed on through generations, become self-fulfilling prophecies as we ironically perpetuate more of the same. The belief creates an energetic frequency of its own, which can repetitively manifest into our lives and the world if we keep telling ourselves the same thing and fail to break the cycle. Thoughts, beliefs, and intentions are so, so powerful—holding onto any of the limiting beliefs mentioned can keep you unconsciously stuck in recurring patterns. As mentioned, it can become a self-fulfilling prophecy! A poverty mindset does not only relate to financial or material abundance, but it also signifies a block in your approach to relationships, love, business opportunities, and following your highest joy and passion.

We all are influenced and affected by our past lives and the karma we create for ourselves, whether we are conscious of it or not. Therefore, it is so important to engage in healing, insight, and guidance from our subconscious.

CUTTING CORDS OF ATTACHMENT

If you feel that you may have old attachments which are holding you back in life, then at some point they need to be addressed and dealt with. These attachments to old, outdated beliefs can conflict with your conscious efforts and willingness to progress in life, across all areas including financial goals or relationship goals to name a few. Changing or altering your belief about an area or thing you want to change or improve in your life is essential for moving forward because if you try and fight the current belief while also trying to move forward it will be like riding a bike with the brakes on.

You may not even be aware of the cords holding you back, as a lot of what goes on behind the scenes is unconscious until we bring it to conscious light. This is done by paying attention to situations where you have a reflex or certain reaction to certain situations which may have different reactions from other people. For example if you dream of being a doctor but know you have to go to university and your first reaction is "I'm not clever enough or too old to go to university", then this would be a belief to consider addressing. Do you really think you are not clever enough, or do you think this because a family member told you or maybe one teacher said this once? Did you always compare yourself to the really clever kids at school and therefore set your bar of intelligence really high which you fell slightly below?

After thinking this through you should then ask yourself whether you know friends who have gone to university that you know for sure did worse than you at school and they got their degree? Or hear about mature students in there 50's who have made the decision to go back to study and they also did good at University. This way of thinking helps question the belief you've held onto for so long and you soon realise that maybe you don't believe you are not clever enough at all!

This process can (and should..) be done across all

areas of your life, you will see the world differently after, like walls have crumbled away.

Once these beliefs have been addressed and you no longer believe what you once did, then you need to push forward with your new belief in place ("I am clever enough), It won't always be easy at first, remember you've held on to the old belief for many many years. As you push forward the new belief becomes stronger and reinforced with time but mostly by new experiences gained by doing things that your old belief never allowed.

Another very common belief is that of money. The association of money and greed, money makes you bad, or rich people and poor people are different and therefore I cannot become rich. Some questions people ask themselves regarding wanting money are:

Am I worthy? Is it immoral to think about and desire money? Do I deserve abundance and financial wealth? Will prosperity change me? Can I be spiritual and heart-centered, and rich and abundant too?

There's nothing wrong with money. Think about it; what do we want money for? To allow us the FREEDOM to do what is important to us, whether this is spending more time with the family, traveling the world, ditching the two-hour commute, not having to answer to a boss, or simply having control of our destiny.

The poverty mindset also manifests as a (very common) belief that there is not enough to go around, and that if you have abundance in wealth, health, love, and happiness, you are taking from another. This is not so. There is more than enough to go around; it is our perceptions that cultivate this faulty belief. Have you heard of the expression "Get out of your own way"?

RAISING YOUR VIBRATIONS

Raising your vibration helps aid the flow of abundance. There is a reason why we often call our interactions and communications with others "vibes." Vibes are the energy we give and project out, and on a spiritual (and scientific) level this is very true and real. We all have an aura or electromagnetic energy field, as briefly touched upon above, so we are all constantly interacting with others on the subtler planes of being. Thoughts and emotions powerfully influence the health and vibratory state of our bodies, minds, and souls, and the external world around us. They also have a great influence on the relationships we keep and social encounters we experience, simply because we literally "give off" and project certain subtle signals, intentions, and messages. The best way to imagine this is like a snake, which can sense things through the vibrations in the ether, or dolphins who communicate telepathically through a supersonic (but completely natural) radar.

How do we raise our vibrations? Declutter your home, declutter your life, address what is bringing your energy down, is it the people around you, the place you work, money, health? It's not necessarily by removing these things but finding a way to confront them and a plan to change the effect they are having on you, the way they make you feel.

Also, find joy in every day. Following your highest joy and true passion(s) is a natural and powerful way to raise your vibration, remove energy blocks, and cut any final lingering cords of attachment and self-destructive ways of thinking, feeling, and relating with others.

CHAPTER 4

DOWNLOADING THE PROGRAMS FROM THE BEGINNING

SO MANY PEOPLE who have managed to harness the true power of the mind have one thing in common—it's the correct mindset. Over the years, you have created your own image of yourself, a mindset that you use in your everyday life. Events in your childhood shaped you to be who you are today, bad or good memories influence you and cloud your eyes. They fill in the empty spots in your heart with doubts about yourself and others around you because it's the way you came to know the world. If you were bullied as a kid, you are probably now insecure and have a poor self-image. But if you grew up to be happy with a lot of attention as a child, you have few or no insecurities. Life is filled with sadness, jealousy, anger, and disappointment, but the good thing is that it's not permanent. You hold the power to change yourself.

CHANGING THE MINDSET

To know what the correct mindset is and how to achieve it, you must first understand what it actually is. A mindset is known to be a self-perception that people hold about themselves, in other words, their beliefs of themselves. Say for example a person thinks that they lack intelligence while another believes that they possess intelligence. This shows that both have a different mindset and understanding of themselves. It is also connected to their personal lives too, saying things like "I'm a bad sister" or "I'm a great mom." Thinking this way has a huge impact on your mindset because it affects the way you act and learn things. If you believe that you are bad at something, then you will find yourself putting little or no effort at all into that particular field.

For example, if you are a student failing a class and you recall putting a lot of effort into your tests and quizzes but you still managed to fail, you begin to doubt your knowledge and yourself, making you less likely to put more effort into something that you believe that you are "bad" at. But another student, who gets good grades and believes that they are able to improve more to reach their desired goals, will put in more effort than usual. People tend to not care when they "realize" that they are bad at something, making them less likely to want to give it another try to improve. They have to be able to change their mindset into thinking that they can improve if they put in a little more effort into their work. We often get discouraged a lot because of other people—a teacher might tell you that they are disappointed in your performance, or a boss might tell you that they were expecting better. This either makes us want to give up or try harder. Those who were doing fine before that one little setback will feel embarrassed that they let someone down, who they deeply respect, while the person who was not doing that well will think that maybe this career path is not for them and might even want to quit. If it's something you believe that you want to do, then go ahead, go try something different, but if you feel as if you don't know if you are making the right decision, then give yourself another chance.

Change up your routine, ask someone for help or guidance. Don't be afraid to reach out to other people for advice. If you always do everything at the last minute, then spread the project out through the entire week. Do at least one hour of it every day—that way you won't have to stress out when you finally reach the deadline. Create a suitable schedule to help you. You have to be able to give yourself another chance, and this time say, "I will do it" because if you go in thinking that "how is this time going to be any different," then you will have doubts from the beginning, thinking that you will never be able to pass that test or make a good quality project. You have to be able to change your mindset and put in all your effort. If you still manage to fail, then this is not what you are supposed to do in the future. We all have a destiny and a path in our lives. If you are uncertain now about what you are planning on doing, then you will figure it out in the future. You will not be sitting on the couch all day and stressing about what you have to do in your life. Go out to places that you enjoy going, look around, and see if there is anything that pulls you towards it. Only you can figure out what you want to do and no one else.

IMPACT OF A NEGATIVE MINDSET

There are countless experiments online which prove that a negative mindset can influence a person poorly. One which caught my attention was where two plants are used; both of them are being cared for equally and for thirty days received equal sunlight and water. One plant receives all the love and positive energy, with words like "I love you" directed at it while the other plant receives no love and negative energy, with words like "I hate you." At the end of the thirty-day challenge, the flower that encountered and absorbed all the negative energy died while the one who absorbed the good energy grew and even bloomed. There was another experiment that took place in a school. Students would come up to the two plants, saying awful things and "bullying" the plant while they would encourage the other one. Both statements were recorded and played to the plants for a period of thirty days. The one who was being bullied died while the other one grew. It shows how powerful our words are to all living things. If it affects a plant, then it definitely affects a person, and it managed to teach the students a valuable lesson. Everything good that you say is taken to heart. It makes people feel good, and it sets their mindset straight, including yours.

Imagine if you were told that you were bad at something, every single day for thirty days. Your mind will be so used to hearing all these things that it will eventually begin to accept the fact that you are bad at this. You tend to give up if people say you aren't good but don't believe them; in fact, make sure to prove them wrong because in this world there are no limits, you can do anything that is physically possible. By believing what others say about you, you will not only let yourself down but also your subconscious mind, which tries so hard to make sure you work hard and your body functions well. You need to let go of those people if you have them in your life—block them out and set your mind straight.

ACCOMPLISHING A POSITIVE MINDSET

Decide on what you want in life and be sure of it. You have to want to accomplish your dreams because you feel that this is something that will bring you joy throughout your life and not because someone else is telling you what to do. The subconscious mind can tell if you are lying or not because it is your own beliefs. If you feel like you want to go and try out a different career path, then go do it. Don't try to manifest your goals if your heart's not in it, it will not work that way.

Focus on the good things in your life. A lot of people say this, but it's the best way to live your best life. If you always think about what you don't have or don't want in your life, you are putting way too much energy into it, making it stick around more. Having a positive mindset will make you more committed to succeeding, which is what will really get you what you want in life. If you want to become a leader, commitment is the strongest quality that a leader can possess, and in order to achieve your goals, you have to stay committed to your work and your process, however slow or fast it may be. Things are not just going to be given to you for free—commitment through success is important. It's not only about motivation; it also requires passion and love for what you do. This will push you to go above and beyond in order to achieve your dreams.

You have to put some action into your goals. You can't learn how to swim from sitting at home and watching videos online. You might be able to get the idea of how to do it but it's not until you actually go out and try it that you actually learn. Act through it. If you sit at home and work from home all day, then it might just feel like you are isolating yourself from the world around you. The universe will provide you with opportunities and people who push you towards your path of success. Don't isolate yourself; otherwise, how they will be able to find you if they can't see you or the work that you do? You need to set your goals straight. If you have doubts, then ask yourself, is your goal something that you really want?

If your goal is to make a lot of money, write a check out to yourself, and even though you don't know how you are planning on achieving it, the ideas will come to you when the time is right. One day you will be hit with a perfect idea on how to make a lot of money, which will shape your path towards success. You have to have an open mindset to all the ideas coming in toward you. Don't be afraid that a lot of days have passed, and you still didn't get anything. You have to be open to all the new possibilities around you and accept that making money will take some more time. Don't stress too much about it and know that it's on the way.

You need to adapt to your surroundings more easily. Sometimes you can't read a book to know how to do something, you have to go out into the world and try things yourself. Perform a safe experiment at home; you learn much better when you go through a process of failure. When you fail, you can also discover other things that you didn't know before. If life puts you into a tough situation, you have to be able to adapt and act quickly; knowing how to control your mind can help you through the process. You don't need to go into a panic and act irrationally because then you won't be able to think straight. You have the right mindset to deal with struggles and pain that the world gives out.

All the successful people in life, whether they have used the power of the mind knowingly or unknowingly, all have one thing in common—they have the right mindset to succeed. They have no doubts or fears and they have a set mindset. A set mindset is when your goals and intentions are set for success. You are able to recognize challenges and face them with no fear because you know that you are going to succeed in life. Life gives us all problems and challenges, but it is up to us to view them as opportunities. There are valuable lessons to be learned from your problems, and even hints to success, so next time something happens to you, take some time to take a step backward and look at the situation from another point of view. What do you see? How can this be a valuable lesson for you? What is it that has caused this to happen? Nothing happens by chance because the universe is always watching and listening to us. Even before you knew of such power, the universe still heard you and sent you things along the way to help and guide you towards your life path. Stop feeling sorry for yourself when life gives you problems. Instead, strive to overcome them because in the future, you will be able to help others in need and tell them your story. Below are some mindsets that are essential to success.

WAYS IN WHICH YOU CAN REPROGRAM YOUR "INNER AUTOPILOT"

They are different, but they can also be complementary; choose the one that best suits your needs and preferences. Proceed with constancy and awareness. The results will be seen soon, and your reality will change forever.

ENVIRONMENTAL INFLUENCES

Have you ever considered the effect of your environment on your subconscious? Your first action is to strictly limit the negativity you are exposed to from now on. Avoid reading negative news and avoid spending too much time with people who could be called "toxic" or negative. Instead, look for positive information to read and absorb, and spend most of your time with positive and successful people. Over time, you will find that more encouraging messages are absorbed into your mind, which will improve the way you see yourself and your potential.

DISPLAY

Your subconscious responds well to images. Visualization is a great way to program your mind with positive and powerful images. Many studies particularly with athletes have shown the power of visualization by causing the brain to think an event is actually happening as it sending signals to the muscles as if the person was actually performing it. The same nerves and muscles were stimulated when the person sat still and visualized or performed the event physically.

STATEMENTS

Affirmations are another effective way to install positive messages into your subconscious mind. As an adult affirmations will need to be repeated over and over until you start to believe them and they become part of your daily vocabulary.

HYPNOSIS

Hypnosis can be effective. The hypnotist gradually speaks to you in a more relaxed and receptive state and provides positive and constructive messages to your subconscious. There is also a more "intimate" version, so to speak, of hypnosis: self-hypnosis. This is a very popular option, where you simply use prerecorded audio instead of live hypnosis sessions. You can even record your own voice, if you think someone else's would distract you; in this way you will be able to hear your voice repeat affirmations or suggestions.

It is important to give this reprogramming time to work. Don't expect to see immediate changes.

Be confident and constant in using these and all the other methods available to reprogram the subconscious. As soon as these transformations become evident, you will feel the motivation to progress, but until that happens, persist. And know that these changes are lasting and powerful.

CHAPTER 5

WHAT HAPPENS AS AN ADULT?

YOUR THOUGHTS and feelings will run amok when you do not have control of your mind. You may find yourself ruminating on things a lot, doubting yourself constantly, or having trouble dealing with your feelings. You should take control of your mind and substitute constructive, specific ones for out-of-control negative thoughts. You'll begin to feel happier, healthier, and in control of your emotions and sense of self over time.

Interestingly, we live in a culture that has created a multitude of ways to alter physical appearance. These ways cover the gamut from clothing, to makeup, hair color, diet, exercise, weightlifting, plastic surgery, etc. Most of us know someone who has markedly altered their physical appearance and provided a lesson as to what is possible.

Mentally, we also have enormous possibilities for change. Through serious study and practice, your mental capabilities can be nurtured and developed. Educational opportunities abound in our modern world. The decision to use these opportunities is up to you. Yet, some are born with serious deficits in their mental capabilities. Although your genetic makeup is the hand you are dealt at birth, it's up to you how you play that hand. Regardless, there are genetic limitations with which we must learn to live and realistic dominant thoughts must consider them.

The question of dominant thoughts changing genetics is quite interesting and beyond the scope of this book. Suffice it to say that there are a multitude of anecdotal examples of people changing physical problems with their mind. The degree to which the changes actually alter genetics has yet to be determined. Yet, it is clear that people have changed the physiological reactions in their body through practiced mental focus. Our control may be much more than is imagined.

Accidents happen to all of us, and we have little or no influence over their occurrence. You drive your car to work and run over a nail, resulting in a flat tire. The flat tire may result in being late to work or a serious automobile accident. For the most part, you have little control over such events. You did decide to drive a car and, therefore, must be prepared to accept the possibility that you may have a punctured tire and the consequences. These possible consequences come with the decision to drive a car. You do have the choice to wear your seat belt, drive defensively, and obey the traffic laws. But even when you take precautions, accidents beyond your control occur.

In all areas of life we are, to some degree, affected by

things beyond our control. We have the choice to take precautions and use good judgment in what we do, but, regardless of all efforts, we are still at the mercy of random events. No amount of mental programming can assure accidents will not happen.

The other thing that we cannot control is other people. However, that we can influence people is a possibility. It is important to recognize the difference.

We say we cannot control people because we recognize that people have free will. A person can choose what they will do. Even when given dire choices, people choose which direction to go. You can threaten a person with firing them, grounding them, beating them, or killing them; yet, even with the threat of death, people can choose for themselves. People are free agents, and, if they are willing to suffer the consequences, they cannot be made to do anything they do not want to do.

Although we cannot control people, we can and do influence people constantly. In the above examples, I described threatening others in order to influence. But this is not the type of influence I want to discuss here. We also influence people in much more subtle ways. The primary way we might have influence on others is through what we say, how we say it, and what we do. Thus, if you want to potentially influence another to change, you must change what you are doing also. And, even if you do change your behavior, there is no guarantee that others will change as a result.

There is an old expression, "You can't change the past, you can't bring back the dead, and you can't make someone love you." Recognizing and avoiding unrealistic objectives is important to creating effective dominant thoughts. This is particularly true with regards to others. When you state your dominant thoughts, make certain that they are directing your behavior and not expected to change something that is out of your control.

Every single one of us has pessimistic feelings all day long. The optimistic essence of our lives, however, is dictated by the truth of how we cope with these negative thoughts. Whether you disregard or embrace them, all is up to your will. If you're not going to stop these negative and unwelcome thoughts, then these negative thoughts will pull you down and even drain you of life and positivity. Throughout our days, we may have endless negative thoughts because we are human beings. But how to stop them in the best possible way is important to think about. At times, we all have pessimistic feelings. When they emerge and then fade away, rage, fear, shame, and other unpleasant emotions are common. However, not only do they make you sad if you get caught in negative thought patterns, they can cause or exacerbate anxiety and depression and can also have a negative effect on things such as your immune system and overall health. Fortunately, to combat negative thoughts, there are steps you can take. In reality, doing so consistently will actually alter the neural pathways in your brain to make you more typically have positive thoughts.

FORMS OF NEGATIVE THOUGHTS

A negative thought can take a variety of forms. Three of the most prevalent are:

OVERANALYZATION

It is prudent to take your time and weigh your options before making significant choices. Evaluating the alternatives, however, may turn into obsessing about them. In order to break this loop, you first have to realize that you are in it. Set a time limit at that stage for making a decision. Give yourself a reasonable amount of time for research and reflection, but then make your decision and stick to it.

RUMINATION NEGATIVE

It is healthy to reflect a certain amount on where you have been and where you are going in life. But that thinking pattern can be very dangerous when those thoughts turn negative, and you spend too much time on them. Starting anything (really, anything) else is a good tactic to avoid rumination. Speaking to a pal. Get a little workout. Work on a hobby of your choosing. Taking action is not "avoiding the problem," but it is a way to place it in the right context instead.

OUTWARD-DIRECTED AGITATION

Whether it's a family member, an acquaintance, or a stranger, we've all been mistreated by someone. In some situations, not only that person but anyone like them may cause us to have a negative opinion of these experiences. We tend to think the worst about people, and those negative feelings may cause us to lash out or withdraw completely when overwhelmed by angry and negative thoughts about others. How do they feel about you? What incentive do they have? What was done to them to make them who they are? It can help you see others in a different, less negative light by pausing to consider these types of questions.

CHANGING YOUR CONSCIOUSNESS

For negative thought, there is no "easy fix." It takes time and commitment to escape harmful thinking patterns and cultivate a fresh outlook on life, but it can be done. Seeing that negative thoughts tend to concentrate on either the past or the future is one thing that can improve. You will stop being caught in regrets or dread by learning to "live in the present moment."

START SMALL

See if, for 30 seconds or a minute, you can concentrate solely on the sensations of one movement. As you wash it, feel the warm water on your face, smell the soap, see how the bubbles shape and pop. You will find that you feel "refreshed" by them when you begin to succeed in keeping your present-moment attention on these kinds of tasks. Extending this exercise to longer and longer times will combat habits of negative thinking and do your state of mind wonders.

ANXIETY IN THE MOMENT

Not only are we concerned about the future, but we are still worried about the things happening around us. But we never know that concern is an expansion of anxiety, and fear in our minds triggers negative thoughts that can pull us down.

THE GUILT OF SOME PAST INCIDENT

Some of us may have done things we're not proud of in our past. We've done something that has been the source of shame before. We did things that didn't turn out the way we expected. Shame about these past errors or mistakes continues to carry our minds to pessimistic thoughts. We need to understand why we believe that no one in the world is OK.

FEAR OF THE FUTURE COMING

Of course, most individuals have a fear of the unknown. People are trying to guess what's going to happen next in life. People are afraid of the future but never think about the reality of what it could offer. Could it earn them a fortune? Uncertainty and thoughts of tragedy and disappointment haunt most average individuals who are anxious about their coming time. It is incredibly important to remember that by worrying about things that have not happened yet or might never happen, we are only wasting our energy and time. It's equivalent to if we were to pay interest on credit cards that we have never actually used in our lives.

There can be many variables in the mind that can cause adverse thinking, but these are some of the more common triggers to remember. Looking at these reasons for keeping negative feelings in mind will assist you in the best way possible to stop them.

HOW ARE NEGATIVE FEELINGS AVOIDED?

You want to avoid negative thoughts? Well, here are some effective tips in this regard that will benefit you.

FIND A DISTRACTION

The fact that a diversion will benefit you is important to consider. But you have to find a diversion that you can use. You can also find a hobby, or you can go shopping for groceries—the thought of something that can catch your attention.

PREFER TO KEEP POSITIVE COMPANY

Go to them if you have a friend or family member with whom you can spend time. Otherwise, reading books can also be an efficient way to hold you away from adverse thoughts.

REFRAME THE STORY WITH CONSTRUCTIVE THOUGHTS

If you can't stop thinking, then reframing your story and thinking about the positivity that you can take from any situation is easier. For starters, if you think your presentation won't go well, think about the trust you're going to gain by facing people.

AVOID JUDGING CIRCUMSTANCES

Mostly, we try to judge all of this on our own. We also continually compare ourselves to those who carry unhappiness. Think that not everyone is comparable, and we all face different circumstances. It is easier to look for beneficial characteristics of the person, circumstance, or yourself.

FEEL GRATEFUL

The easiest way to keep yourself away from negative feelings is to cultivate appreciation. Studies have shown that feeling grateful can have a great effect on levels of positivity and satisfaction. Remember the things that are going well and feel their satisfaction instead of worrying more about the adverse circumstances. Promoting positivity is one of the most powerful ways to keep away from negative feelings and experience more happiness.

CHAPTER 6

BELIEFS CREATE YOUR REALITY

YOU WERE NOT BORN with somebody else's beliefs; you developed and acquired them all over time. As a consequence, you may alter an older belief or obtain a new one. This doesn't suggest you can merely challenge your impressions, and you will dwell on thoughts. The famous aphorism "Nature abhors a vacuum" is remarkably accurate in your mind. If you remove an older opinion, it creates a void that begs to be filled.

That is why you have to select and put in a brand-new belief to take the place of this older one. Imagine you could visit the shop and get any notion you desired, as though it were a bit of software, which you can take home and install on your PC. You can, metaphorically speaking. That computer is the mind, and it is ready and waiting to take any new applications you select. So, ask yourself what beliefs could be useful for you to install on your computer.

One of the biggest lies we humans choose to accept is

that our beliefs are facts. We all want to think our opinions, convictions, and views accurately reflect reality, that what we believe in is true. No one likes to be wrong.

Our beliefs greatly influence our emotions and actions, and we use them to understand and navigate the world. Many researchers would agree that the majority or our core and fundamental beliefs are formed by the age of six. Generally, these beliefs are formed in two ways: through our own experiences and by accepting what others tell us to be true.

Once formed, our beliefs become embedded in us. And they play a critical role in shaping the direction of our lives. Regardless of whether they are actually true or not, we live as if they are factual. Our beliefs determine if we consider something to be good or bad, right or wrong, beautiful or ugly, safe or dangerous, or acceptable or unacceptable. Beliefs influence our decisions—whether we choose to follow our dreams or accept mediocrity, complain or take action, hit the gym or spend the evening on the couch. Beliefs matter.

But how can we give so much credit to something that by its very definition is not a fact? If we look at the dictionary definition, nowhere will you find the word "fact." Instead, it is defined as:

An acceptance that a statement is true or that something exists. A firmly held opinion or conviction.

Even if multiple people agree on it, a belief is only a thought in the mind that we have thought long enough to the point where we accept it as true. There is no need to be attached to any of them or be convinced they are true.

We don't even need to accept them, especially those that don't serve us. You are as capable as you want to be. You are as worthy as you think.

So often we pass up potential opportunities because we allow the mind to tell us we "can't." This is your conscious mind operating on fears developed from past experiences and other people's belief systems.

HOW TO USE YOUR BELIEF STRATEGY TO REMOVE FEAR

Fear is often considered by many in the self-help industry to be the enemy of success. Great rewards are obtained from taking risks in life. If fear often reigns within you, you'll never have the courage to take risks, and you'll have a very difficult time accomplishing anything great.

Experiencing natural fear from time to time is part of life. It is a normal thing, but it can be physically and emotionally weakening if you live with constant fear. You won't be able to live your life to the fullest if you keep on refusing to join various daily activities just because you might have to face your fear of social interaction.

Even the bravest people in the world have certain fears that they have had to overcome. It doesn't really matter whether you're afraid of heights, spiders, failure, or change as long as you're courageous enough to accept, confront, and take control of your fears to keep them from restraining you, when it comes to the things you want to do most in your life.

Sooner or later, you may start to acquire new fears

unconsciously, but you shouldn't dwell on them but should make it a priority to unlearn those new fears as well. It's important not to deny having such fears and being aware of them is also essential, as you begin the first step toward eradicating them. Anyone can learn how to overcome fear. It's a skill. People usually just cling to them because their fears are a part of their entire disposition. There's nothing wrong if you feel like you're not yet ready to face your fears, but you will know when it is the right time.

ANALYZE AND EVALUATE YOUR FEARS

ACKNOWLEDGE YOUR FEARS

Ignoring or denying the fact that you have fears, even to yourself, is a very easy thing to do, especially when you want to appear brave or strong to others. The truth is, you can't really consider yourself as brave if you aren't able to accept the fact that you have fears in the first place.

Acknowledging your feelings is the first step in taking control over the situation. Write down on a sheet of paper, "I (insert name), am currently afraid of (insert fear), and I will overcome this fear because I want to accomplish....."

IDENTIFY YOUR FEARS

Sometimes fear can be easily recognized, but other times you can't even explain where those anxious feelings are coming from. Learn to name your fears. What is it exactly that makes you so afraid? Once you understand what your fears are about, you're already on your way towards eliminating them.

Journaling can be a good way to keep track of your progress while you're striving to overcome your fears. Write down every fear that bothers you. Oftentimes when I have written down the fears that I have, I have started to realize that these fears only existed in my head and the chance of the occurrence actually happening in reality was slim to none.

IDENTIFY THE STRUCTURE

Dealing with your fear and considering it as something that has a beginning and an end can surely help you realize that you have control over it. Delve into its roots. When, where, and how did it begin? Did it start with a traumatic experience? Does it have anything to do with your childhood environment at school or home? How long have you been afraid of said thing? What triggers it and how does it affect you?

Fear is sometimes a healthy emotion that can protect you from harm or doing something silly. Find out whether you have a really good, realistic reason to possess this fear or if it is simply inhibiting.

IMAGINE YOUR DESIRED OUTCOME

As soon as you understand and recognize your fear, think about the things you want to change. Your main goal might be to overcome all of your limiting fears in life, but keep in mind that it is important to establish smaller, measurable goals to achieve success in the long term.

Do it one step at a time. Imagine the person that you will be once you overcome the issues that you have right now and think about how beneficial it will be once you get there.

TAKE CHARGE OF YOUR FEARS

GRADUALLY LESSEN SENSITIVITY

Usually, people are afraid of things because they haven't correctly been exposed to them. We commonly describe it as "fear of the unknown." Try to expose yourself, little by little, to the things that you're afraid of, until you learn to understand them better and your fear of them will start to dissolve.

TRY DIRECT CONFRONTATION

Sometimes, the best way to overcome your fears is to confront them, face to face. When you encounter the cause or basis of your fears, you might realize that there's really nothing to be afraid of and that you've just made up all those scary scenarios in your head. Imagination can make reality look terrifying if it gets out of control. Once you've decided to take action, your fears become weaker, and the new reality isn't as bad as you'd originally thought it would be.

LEARN TO HANDLE FAILURE

Facing your own fears can be quite difficult and challenging, and you don't always end up triumphant right away. You may have to face them many times before you can actually say that you've defeated your fears for good. You must make it a point to remember why you started on this journey in the first place.

Focus on how helpless you'll feel if you let the fear defeat you in the long run. This thought will help to drive you when times get tough. Remember that failure is only a stepping-stone on the road to your success. The world won't end when you fail at something, but your fear will stay scary if you quit and let it be that way for good.

DON'T STOP THE MOMENTUM

Always remember that nothing is impossible when you're absolutely determined to achieve your goals. Perseverance is the key in getting past your fears. Don't worry about how much progress you made each day, just make sure that you are making progress over time. You should be trending upward.

MINDFULNESS

The word "mindfulness" seems to be everywhere these days. If you are like most people, you might even be confused about what it actually means. Some might think mindfulness is a spiritual practice while others know nothing about it. The truth is that mindfulness is not nearly as complicated as the mainstream media makes it seems. In reality, the act of mindfulness simply refers to the mental state of being present. It is both a practice and a way of being in every moment of life. When you practice mindfulness, your goal is to train your brain to experience the essence of the current situation. The reason you need to use mindfulness in your everyday life is that our mind is a natural time traveling portal. Because of this, most of us spend a lot of our mental energy and time thinking about future and past events. We are either worrying about events that are coming up and how we'll react to them, or we're constantly thinking about something that already happened and how we should have dealt with it. Even though this behavior is natural, it can be quite detrimental to our mental and physical health.

You see, when you are constantly thinking about upcoming events, you put your mind in a state of perpetual prediction. What you need to realize is that no one knows the future; you can't tell what's going to happen tomorrow, next week, or even two hours from now. But our brains have adapted to make us focus on the possibilities of the future. This is because, in the past, our hunter-gatherer ancestors lived in a danger-filled natural environment. So, the mind adapted to predicting the future in order to help us be more conscious of any perceived danger. The problem nowadays is that we no longer live in that environment, but our brains have not changed. That is why most of us can't stop our minds from wondering all the time. If this behavior persists, it can lead to anxiety and panic attacks.

On the other hand, when your mind is trapped in the past, it increases your chances of suffering from depression. When we ruminate about the past, we often focus on what we should have done or said. This leaves the door wide open for feelings of regret and guilt. But even if you are thinking about good memories of the past, doing this could make you start comparing your current state with the past feelings you had. While it's important that you plan for the future and learn from the past, the problem we're facing is that we can't seem to let go of the thoughts and enjoy being in the present. This is where practicing mindfulness meditation can drastically improve our lives by helping us gain mental clarity.

When you are mindful, you notice the events that are currently happening in your head and around you. Some people might feel fearful about paying attention to the present, but there is nothing to worry about. The act of mindfulness teaches us how to enjoy our emotions and immerse ourselves in whatever we're feeling regardless if it's negative or positive. In essence, what mindfulness does is that it gives us the power to slow down our minds. Instead of spending our mental energy thinking about possible events, we are consciously choosing to experience our thoughts and emotions as they are happening to us. Science says that the brain is the most energy-consuming organ in the body. It uses up to 20% of the body's total energy supply. When your mind is constantly entertaining too many thoughts, you feel weak because your brain is being overworked. Our ancestors didn't have much to worry about. All they needed was food, shelter, a sexual partner, and maybe some clothes. They lived in small communities with a handful of people. So, their minds could afford to wander. But we live in a very distracted world. On any given day, we have a million things that are seeking our attention. There is the news, social media, meetings, kids, fashion, and so much more. If you can't keep your mind calm, you will easily become overwhelmed. The worst part is that because we are exposed to so much information, sometimes we don't know what is making us feel the way we do. For instance, maybe on your way to work, you hear on the radio that your favorite show got canceled. Now, this is not a big deal, but unknowingly to you, this information has triggered thoughts of anger in your mind. So, when your colleague said something slightly offensive, you'd find yourself overreacting to the situation. Without knowing it, you've allowed your emotions about your favorite show being canceled to influence your relationship with your coworker. While this may seem strange, most of us can relate to such situations.

Our minds have become so noisy that they tend to move swiftly from one thought to another and from one time frame to the next. One minute you are thinking about what you will have for lunch, and before you notice it, you're angry about what your partner said the other day. There are some days when it will feel like your brain is spinning out of control. What mindfulness will do for you is help you disconnect yourself from your thoughts and emotions by slowing down the pace that you're experiencing them. You'll become present and begin to observe without judgment what is happening around you and in your mind. It will also help you stop attaching meaning to your experiences without first understanding them. This doesn't mean that you will become a mindless blurb or a Zen master overnight. Rather, you are opening your mind to enjoying the magic of the moment. Mindfulness meditation helps you take control of the intertwined emotions that you feel. This means that when you practice mindfulness meditation, you are saying enough of the chaos in your head, and you're taking back your mind with kindness and curiosity.

CHAPTER 7

HERE COMES THE RESISTANCE

WE'VE ALL HEARD IT, the saboteur—that little voice inside your head that keeps telling you that you can't do something. It's a voice that tells you something is too hard, or it is impossible. It whispers in your ear that what you are trying to do is ridiculous. It tells you to listen to reason and to quit dreaming about things that you will never have. It is a voice that you need to learn to quiet. You need to learn how to shut it out, and how to replace it with an attitude that tells you that you can reach your goals.

Will it be easy to quiet the saboteur? Unfortunately, the answer to this is no. It's hard to shut that little voice out, but it's not impossible. While there will be days where the saboteur gets the better of you, it's up to you to limit these days. It's up to you to find a way to contain that little voice, and once you do, all of your hopes, goals, and dreams will become possible.

So, where does the saboteur come from? Why do we

all have a negative voice within our own minds that tries to hold us back from reaching our goals and dreams?

The saboteur is the result of the influence that society has upon us. Over the course of our lives, society exerts its influence upon us. It tries to mold us into what is considered to be the norm. Many of the people that surround us have given up on their hopes and dreams, and they try to get us to do the same.

The accumulated effect of the influences in our lives gives rise to the saboteur. If you allow it to, the saboteur can keep you from trying to reach your goals and dreams. It has the power to alter the course of your life and prevent you from reaching the extraordinary. The saboteur can change you; it can force you to compromise and accept that it's okay to give up on what you want.

The problem with the saboteur is that it's always there. It's always whispering to you that it's okay to give up. It tells you that you should just be like everyone else. It tries to convince you that it's okay to be ordinary. The saboteur is a powerful force that can leave you disappointed and unhappy with the life that you have lived.

If you want to overcome the influence of the saboteur, you need to realize that it has no power over you. You do this by accepting that taking risks and choosing the more difficult path isn't just all right, it's necessary. When you fail at something, the saboteur is there telling you that you shouldn't try any more. What you need to do is ignore this little voice and then get back up and keep trying. It's not always easy, but few things in life that are truly worth attaining are easy.

The saboteur lives in your subconscious mind, it controls you without you even realising that it's happening. That's why the saboteur is such a powerful force. It's that constant negative voice whispering to you that it's impossible. You can't do it, you will fail. Just give up. It will force you to give in and conform to what everyone else expects of you if you let it.

The worst part about the saboteur is that it's telling you what most of the people in your life are probably already telling you. Because of this, the saboteur makes sense, it speaks to you with the sound logic that taking the safer path is the smart way to go. But the problem with this is that it forces you to give up on your hopes and dreams. Nobody ever became a race car driver by playing it safe. But just about everyone who goes to work and spends their day sitting behind a desk has taken the safe path. What you need to realize is that the saboteur wants the kind of life for you that will ultimately leave you unhappy.

If you want to reach the goals and dreams that you have set for yourself, you need to find a way to quiet and control the saboteur. Every time that little voice tells you that you can't do something, you need to fight it. You need to resist its influence or you will be doomed to fail.

It's easy to listen to the saboteur. It's easy because it's telling you to do what logic says is the smarter choice. It's telling you to try to get a nice, safe, steady job instead of shooting for the stars. It's the part of your mind that wants you to make the safer choices so that you minimize risk. The problem with minimizing risk is that you also minimize the potential rewards you could see. If you don't fight for your dreams, then they won't come true. If this happens, the saboteur will have won, and you will be left with a lot of lingering questions and regret.

For people who strive to attain what others call impossible, each day can be a struggle. A struggle not only against the influence that people around you have upon you, but also against your own lingering self-doubt. Self-doubt that takes the form of the ever present and persistent voice of the saboteur. Don't try it, the saboteur tells you. It's not going to work. You'll look foolish when this fails. You need to give up on this nonsense and face reality. What you really need to do is to shut this voice up any way that you can.

Fighting for your hopes and dreams takes a lot of character strength. It will take dedication on your part and the ability to silence the critics that seek to stop you. This means that you need to silence what may be the toughest critic of all, the lingering doubt within your own mind, known as the saboteur.

DEFEATING THE SABOTEUR

The saboteur may end up becoming the single greatest threat that you have to face in order to reach your goals and dreams. It's not always easy to shut out the negative thoughts and opinions that others have and share with you. It's even more challenging to shut out those same types of negativity when it is coming from your own subconscious mind.

What you need to realize is that even though it's your own internal voice, the saboteur does not represent who you are. It isn't your true self. Instead, the saboteur is the result of the negativity and defeatist attitude that you have been exposed to from a young age. It's everyone that has ever shot down your dreams or told you that something was impossible. It's the parent who looked at you as a child and told you that you shouldn't try to become a race car driver or singer because it's too hard.

Because of how strongly ingrained the voice of the saboteur can be into your core personality, it's influence can be truly imposing. The good news is that despite its strength, you can defeat the power that the saboteur has over you.

The first step in defeating the saboteur is to recognize where it gets its strength from. While it may speak to you in your own voice, it's simply channeling the voices of everyone who has ever told you that you can't achieve something. Once you recognize where the saboteur comes from, you can start to learn to resist it.

You see, it's not really your own self-doubt that you need to overcome. It is the doubt that has been instilled within you by others. Deep down you really want to be happy and successful. Deep down you really do believe in yourself and think that you can achieve your goals and dreams. The key to being able to listen to your positive thoughts is to learn to shut out the negative influence of the saboteur.

Once you recognize what the saboteur truly is, you can then start to look for ways to neutralize its influence over you. Whenever the nagging voice of the saboteur tries to control you, try to think of where it's coming from. Recognize that it's not your voice that is telling you to give up, it's voices of others.

Try to remember the people that have had influences upon you and then think about how those people affected you. The saboteur was born from the negativity in your life that you were exposed to from a young age. Unfortunately, it's often the negative experiences that we remember more than the positive ones.

You can probably tell your friends about a time you were treated poorly, even if it happened many years ago. You can probably describe the incident in great detail. However, you probably don't have the same type of clear memories of positive events. Because negative experiences and influences are able to more strongly influence most people, the voice of the saboteur becomes strong and hard to resist.

Since the saboteur is the result of the negativity that you have been exposed to, the best way to overcome it is to replace its bad influence upon you with a positive one. Will it be easy to silence this damaging and destructive little voice? It shouldn't come as a surprise to you that it won't be.

The saboteur has lived in your subconscious mind and has been an influence fighting against you reaching your hopes and dreams for many years. It has thrived and fed upon the self-doubt that has been inflicted upon you by every negative person you have ever encountered. It has sat there hidden in the dark resources of your mind and subtly influenced your decision-making process by making you question your convictions and abilities.

Instead of trying to silence the saboteur, you should instead try to figure out how to reprogram it. You need to find a way to turn its negativity into a positive voice that can encourage you instead of discouraging you. You do this by first fighting the saboteur's negative influence each time it tries to keep you from pursuing what you truly want. Each time that little voice tells you that something is impossible, you need to quiet it. You need to tell it that it's wrong, and most importantly, you need to tell it why. You need to believe in yourself and be able to tell the saboteur that it's wrong and that you are right.

One of the best ways that you can fight the saboteur and successfully reprogram it is by committing your thoughts to paper. Much like writing down your dreams is important, so is writing down your reasons for believing in these dreams. Make a list of the positive qualities that you have that you feel are important in helping you to reach your goals. Keep this list with you, and look at it whenever you begin to doubt yourself.

Whenever the saboteur begins to whisper in your ear that you can't do something, fight back by thinking about why you can do it. It won't be easy. It also won't be quick. But over the course of time, you can get yourself to the point where you don't need the list anymore to resist the power of the saboteur. As you continue to gain strength, you can stop resisting the saboteur, and instead, defeat it by turning its negativity into a positive force that will benefit you in all walks of life.

You can defeat the saboteur. It's going to take time and a lot of effort, but it's definitely possible. When you look around at the truly successful people in the world, do you think that they let self-doubt slow them down? Do you think that they have accomplished all that they have by listening to the voice of the saboteur? Or do you think that they overcame it, that they reprogrammed it and now it is a voice that serves them?

Well, if you chose the latter, you are correct!

CHAPTER 8

AWARENESS

VALUES ARE WHAT MATTER. Ask yourself: "What do I consider important?" The answer will reflect your ideas about what you consider to be genuine, what you are convinced of, what you believe in. We often use the concepts of "value system" and "belief system" as synonyms. For example, the words: "I believe that being honest is very important" (value) practically means "I believe in honesty" (conviction). Sometimes, the connections are not so straightforward: "The bosses care only about themselves" (persuasion) coexists with the idea: "You must care first and foremost about your interests" (implied value) or: "We must end racial discrimination in this organization" (persuasion based on the value of universal equality).

Beliefs and values are formed within us throughout life. As filters of thought, they exert a relentless influence on any idea of the external world, thus affecting all the results we have outlined and decisions made. In short, they completely control our lives, become motives for actions, determine our achievements. They affect the way we perceive ourselves (our individuality) and develop as individuals. They help us build an individual map of the world and reality.

IDENTIFICATION OF VALUES

You can relate your values to the specific goals outlined in the second lesson. Ask yourself: "Why is this result important to me? In what circumstances and situations?" It can be beneficial to apply these questions to various areas of your life, which helps you not to forget about less obvious goals. In this process, you can identify conflicting values that are related, for example, to work and personal life. Such questions often bring to the surface what you have felt for a long time. Think, for example:

- about your work and career;
- about your family;
- about your social life;
- about your hobbies;
- about your interests;
- about your self-development;
- about spiritual needs and about your mission; and
- other areas of life that you can highlight.

In particular, with regard to work, you can ask yourself, for example, such questions: "What is important for me as a nurse's career (accountant, plumber, etc.)?" or: "Why is working at XYZ Limited important to me?" The answers can be: "stability," "respect for others," "communication with people," "the ability to help others," "earnings," etc. These answers will reflect your values. Try to keep the answer as concise as possible.

The very need to find the right word can make you seriously rethink this element of the value system. Some words will begin to be repeated, and very soon, you will make a list of your values.

HIERARCHY OF VALUES

Looking through the list of values, on each of them ask yourself the question: "Why do I consider this important?" Answers may include other values that you did not initially think about. At the same time, you will clarify the already identified values—and soon, you will be able to feel a certain hierarchy in them and arrange them in order of importance.

You can evaluate the importance of values with a simple question: "Which of them do I consider the most important?" Having selected some of them, ask the same question in relation to those listed in the remaining paragraphs. In the end, you will get an ordered list. Clarify the hierarchy by comparing neighboring items: "What is more important, this or this?" For example, what is "honesty" in relation to "fidelity" for you? Soon you will finally be able to arrange the values in a hierarchy of their importance.

You may find that it is most difficult to deal with so-called nominalizations: abstract concepts such as "independence" or "reliability." To clarify their importance, try formulating questions in a specific context. For example: "What would I choose if I could choose between a job that provides independence vs. a stable position?" Imagine both options, and an intuitive answer will confirm the importance of the values being compared. It helps the mind focus.

The same questions can be applied to your hobbies and all other areas of life. Soon there will be a certain pattern, as common values apply to all spheres of human life. Regardless of the size of the list, only a few critical values influence whether you achieve your goals and how you do it. Now, you can make practical use of the list: compare the values listed in it with the correctly formulated results set in the second lesson and, for each goal, ask yourself the question: "Is it consistent with my values?"

WHERE DO THE VALUES COME FROM?

Having determined your values, you can identify their source. How did they come about? Under the influence of your family or friends, religion, school, place of residence, financial situation, media, teacher, or another person whom you respect?

You can find other sources of your values. In some cases, they can be associated with a specific person ("I will never forget what she told me ...") or time and place

("The moment that this happened, I decided that ..."). Although the circumstances of the emergence of values are not so important for the process of their change, the determination of the source often confirms the random nature of their origin, and at times the small importance of a particular value for your current goals. On the other hand, the "pedigree" of a value can, on the contrary, emphasize its importance in the current circumstances. In short, the value system provides you with a wide range of choices. You can change it as you wish. If you can align your goals with the hierarchy of values, then you will increase the chances of achieving the intended results.

EVALUATION

At some point in your life, you may have been evaluated by someone to let you know how well or how poorly you performed on a given assignment or job. It may have been a written evaluation, verbal, or a combination of both. Just about every corporation or business conducts evaluations, reviews, or performance appraisals on their employees, similar to the kind my first employer used with me.

These evaluations are used to determine eligibility for jobs, advancement, bonuses, and salary increases. They are also used to evaluate your performance on the job and your value to the company.

Additionally, you may discuss any future goals you may have that will be of benefit to the company as well as the company's goals and the role you will play to meet them.

These evaluations especially allow the employer, usually an immediate supervisor or manager, an opportunity to conduct a face-to-face session with the employee to let them know exactly what they think of them and their job performance. Sometimes the evaluation matches how the employee feels they have performed, but more often than not, the employee feels they have performed better than their employer's appraisal.

These types of evaluations are usually forced upon the employee as a requirement of employment. They are conducted by other people, using standards and measures they have developed. And while I benefited greatly from the evaluations provided by my employer, I never had or knew of anything else I could use to evaluate my Self with.

So, the question is: What tool are you using to evaluate your Self? How do you evaluate your current state of being? What standards do you use to determine your performance at work, at home, in your personal relationships, or in managing your money? In evaluating your health or level of education? In evaluating your ability to resolve issues related to the most important matters in your life?

Are you setting goals to improve your Self in any of these areas? Are you using anything to provoke new thoughts and ideas regarding your personal life or future? Are you currently using anything to conduct periodic evaluations on your Self to determine if you are taking responsibility for your life and the situations you are creating?

If not, the TEST is exactly what you need. And if the answer is yes, the TEST can serve as an additional tool, a helpful option that can be used to validate and complement what you are already using. The Process of Evaluation contained in this book is for your use, not your employer's.

The TEST is a tool for you to evaluate your Self and the lifestyle you are living. It will provoke the thoughts and ideas that are necessary for you to understand your Self better and create a lifestyle of your own choosing; to create a life filled with peace, happiness, and success in whatever it is you choose to pursue.

These three requirements will help you identify areas of your thinking and behavior that may require a change. And you will discover that the areas where change will most commonly be required will be in your beliefs, environment, actions, conditioning, or habits.

This is your opportunity to look in the mirror and see the real you; the you that is hidden from everyone else because it resides within you. The evaluations conducted on you by corporations, businesses, and other people document what they feel about you—their perception of you.

And while these evaluations serve an important function, only you can perform an honest and true evaluation of your Self.

"Self" has been purposefully separated from "'yourself" because it is a separate entity within you; it is your inner being, your consciousness, that thinking part of you or the voice in your head. This is the part of you that will undergo the evaluation. The you that nobody else knows or sees; the you that's reading this book. Because this is where real change has to begin—within your Self.

The TEST is also an actual test. It is a test to see if you are willing to do the work that is necessary to complete a thorough evaluation of your Self as well as the situations you have created in your life. You will easily pass this test if you answer all of the questions, complete all of the quizzes, and complete all of the exercises presented to you.

And yes, I hear you...not another test! Those are the words that come to mind anytime I'm asked to answer questions for a test, exam, or evaluation. But I have come to realize that tests serve a very important purpose. Tests evaluate something to see where it stands today; not tomorrow but now, at this moment in time. Tomorrow's results could be different.

Tests give us a point of reference, a standard that we can use to determine if some type of correction or change is needed. And let's face it, you never know the truth about your Self, your level of knowledge, how you respond under pressure, and so many other things until you put your Self to the test, until you look in the mirror and evaluate your Self as no one else can. This book, the TEST, provides you with that very thing.

You will evaluate your Self by using four Personal Development Solutions. These will be covered in greater detail shortly. Each Personal Development Solution contains information that is used for your Self-evaluation as well as evaluating the situations you have created. This is where the work must be completed in order to pass the test.

You will do exceptionally well in completing a thorough evaluation of your Self as well as pass the test if you answer all of the questions, complete all exercises, and complete each quiz contained in the Personal Development Solutions. Again, this is for your benefit. If you are not ready to put the time in to complete the work, the Personal Development Solutions will be of no benefit to you, and you will not pass the test.

But more importantly, you will miss out on the opportunity to bring clarity into your thinking regarding your Self and the situations in which you are participating.

Reading The Evaluation of Self-Test is easy. Completing the work and changing your Self and the situations you are creating will be the hardest part of the process. It can be difficult for some people to answer questions about how they think and feel or assess their strengths and weaknesses. Changing any aspect of your thoughts, emotions, and behavior can be a constant struggle.

Keep this in mind as you read through the book: it's not about seeking perfection. Your goal should be to bring order into each area of your life if and where it does not already exist. This should ultimately bring more happiness and peace into your life.

Your Self-evaluation will be like the *Portrait of Dorian Gray*. In the movie of the same title, Dorian's portrait reflects the pain of his life on his face, in monstrous detail. The results of your Self-evaluation, your test results, may paint an unflattering picture of you and the life you are living.

It is my hope that it will paint a pretty picture or one that only needs a little touch-up. But there will not be a picture if you don't provide honest answers during the Self-evaluation process.

PERSONAL DEVELOPMENT

One of the goals of this book is to help you develop into the person you want to become while living a lifestyle that brings you peace, happiness, and success in whatever you choose to undertake. This goal will be achieved when you complete your Self-evaluation and take the action that is necessary for you to improve in any area of your life you feel is lacking or deficient.

But in order for this to occur and this Self-evaluation to be a success, a personal choice has to be made by you to complete it. Going into this halfheartedly will not be of benefit to you so make your decision now. No one is forcing this on you so the choice is yours.

But by continuing to read this book, you will have decided to change something about your Self. You will have decided to develop into the kind of person that takes control of their thoughts, actions, and behavior.

Again, please don't fool your Self into thinking this will be easy. A real, long-term commitment of your time and energy is required here. You must plant the seeds of knowledge provided in the form of Personal Development Solutions into your thoughts, so they can grow and become a part of your mindset, your lifestyle, and your day-to-day living.

True change has to occur in the mind first— in your "Self." You can change a hundred things outside of your Self and not see or feel like any real change has occurred in your life. Hundreds if not thousands of people lose weight from dieting and exercise every year. But a large percentage of them still think and view themselves as being overweight.

They lost the weight but did not lose the overweight thought or image they had within their Self. This is one of the many reasons people gain the weight back. But by changing what's inside of you first, your Self, your thoughts and images (internally), it will be much easier to change anything outside of your Self (externally). This is the type of change that can last a lifetime.

PERSONAL DEVELOPMENT SOLUTIONS

They will take you on a journey through your Self. They are the tools by which you will evaluate your Self. They will help you evaluate your thoughts and feelings which have been dictating your actions. With this knowledge in hand, you can then evaluate your actions which have over time, determined your behavior.

Once you can clearly see what your behavior has been, you will be in a better position to evaluate your attitude towards life, your life situations, and the world around you like you have never seen it before.

The success of your Self-evaluation and your future

development will depend greatly on your ability to apply the knowledge you gain from the Personal Development Solutions to your internal Self and the external situations you are involved in.

There are four Personal Development Solutions presented. They are:

- Knowing Your Purpose
- Understanding Your Life Situation
- Understanding the Importance of Setting Goals
- Living a Balanced Life

Each Solution provides you with valuable thought-provoking information to make you more aware of your current situation and what is necessary to change any aspect of it.

You must answer all of the questions on each quiz to ensure you have absorbed the information. These quizzes will also help stimulate the creative ideas that are necessary for you to make important decisions about your Self and your life so that you can start planning your future.

The following is a brief description of each Personal Development Solution that you will evaluate your Self with.

KNOWING YOUR PURPOSE

We start your evaluation by determining if you know what your purpose is. You will determine what the purpose of your existence is as a creative being. This will establish what the focus of your internal state of being, your Self, is or will be.

Everything else you do after creating this statement will be focused on helping you to achieve it. Thus, you must create a purpose statement before continuing to the next Personal Development Solution.

Your purpose will be your starting point, or rather, your point of reference from where the many choices and decisions you will need to make will emanate from as you move forward through your Self-evaluation. All of your thoughts and actions must be in agreement with the purpose you choose for your Self.

UNDERSTANDING YOUR LIFE SITUATION

Your life situation is the result of the many choices and decisions you have made in the past and what you think about them as a whole. It includes all the situations you have created or are involved in, such as your job situation, your health situation, your financial situation, your marital situation, or the situation with your coworker, neighbor, or friend, etc. It is basically everything you might be thinking about if you are not focused on what is happening in the present moment.

You will evaluate the many situations you are

currently involved in and determine which ones are problem free, need improvement and which, if any, are continually problematic. You will also evaluate your beliefs, environment, actions, conditioned responses, and habits related to the situations in your life. You will then create a philosophy that will establish a plan of action by which you act and behave based on your findings and your unique life situation.

Your plan of action will establish the principles by which you use the creative force within you to change any situation that needs improvement, is continually problematic, or is not in alignment with your purpose. Your philosophy will also provide the direction and guidance you need to create new situations that are in alignment with your purpose as you move forward.

A complete understanding of the situations you are currently involved in is one of the most important factors in your evaluation. Your current life situation and your thoughts and feelings about it will determine if or where a need for change exists.

UNDERSTANDING THE IMPORTANCE OF SETTING GOALS

This Personal Development Solution will determine if you understand the importance of setting goals. You will evaluate if you know what goals are, how to create them, and what their importance is in your personal development and the process of change.

You will also learn how to create a Measurable

Action Plan (MAP). It will serve as your written plan of action to achieve your goals. The MAP will list all of the goals you decide upon to change your Self and your life situations. Your MAP will always be available as needed to guide you during those periods when you lose your way or forget what you are trying to achieve and the reason why. You may follow the example below of a MAP planner, and also refer to the questions presented in the section: *Take Responsibility and Ownership for Your Life* .

7 DAY MAP PLANNER

Outcome:		
Motivation:		
7 Day MAP Planner		
Monday	Activity:	Goal:
Tuesday	Activity:	Goal:
Wednesday	Activity:	Goal:
Thursday	Activity:	Goal:
Friday	Activity:	Goal
Saturday	Activity:	Goal:
Sunday	Activity:	Goal

LIVING A BALANCED LIFE

And finally, the last solution is Living a Balanced Life. You will evaluate if you are living a balanced life based on the definition provided. We will also discuss the Five Points of Balance. They are the means by which you can achieve a defined state of balance.

These points focus on what happens inside of you; in your thoughts, in your body's reaction to these thoughts by way of your feelings and emotions, and finally the impact that these thoughts, feelings, and emotions have on your life situations.

One of the most important of these points is Self-Induced Obstacles. As you begin to change and develop into the person you want to be, Self-Induced Obstacles will begin to surface. We will review this and other obstacles and provide ideas on how to remove or reduce their impact on your Self, your life, and your ability to live in, or close to, a perfect state of balance.

EVALUATION POINTS

These are your four Personal Development Solutions. They serve as your evaluation tool and your test. Each solution contains evaluation points for you to examine, measure, analyze, explore, and evaluate your Self by.

These solutions will help you begin the process of change that leads to your development into the person you desire to be, living a lifestyle of your choosing. You will complete a thorough evaluation of your Self and your life situation by doing the following:

Consider every question that is asked in the Personal Development Solutions, including quizzes, an evaluation point.

Pause for a moment or two to assess how each question may relate to you mentally (thoughts), physically, emotionally, or spiritually (feelings).

Give extra time and consideration to questions or areas that are identified as important evaluation points.

The completion of every exercise should be considered an evaluation point.

These are the procedures you should follow to complete your evaluation. This is where the work must be done. This is where you discover if or where change is needed. And this is what will determine if you will pass the test.

If you find your Self reading through the pages without reflecting for a moment or two on a question you were asked or skipping exercises and leaving answers to quiz questions blank, you are wasting your time. Your evaluation will be incomplete. At this point, you should stop, put the book down and begin again when you feel you are ready to do the work.

Jim Rohn, the great motivational speaker said, "Work harder on your Self than you do on your job" (SUCCESS Staff, 2017). If you work hard at completing this evaluation, just as you would an assignment at your job, you will build an understanding of your Self that will propel you to heights you never thought you could reach. You will reap all of the benefits and rewards in the same manner as I did from the evaluations performed on me by my first employer.

So, it is my hope that you are ready, willing, and able to complete your evaluation and in the end, pass the test. But before we begin, there is one more thing you must be ready to do.

TAKE RESPONSIBILITY AND OWNERSHIP FOR YOUR LIFE

As I said earlier, true change occurs in the mind first. Accepting the truth about what is occurring in your life and taking full responsibility and ownership in changing whatever it is that you are tired of tolerating, is the beginning of a change of mind. Until you take full responsibility for what has occurred or is occurring within your Self and your life, true change cannot happen.

One of the first things Alcoholics Anonymous requires participants to do is to accept they are alcoholics by saying, "Hello, my name is Jim and I'm an alcoholic." You must take responsibility for the situations you have created by saying to your Self, "My name is Jim and I made the choices and decisions that have led me to my current state of being, and I either created or chose to participate in the situations I am involved in, and I am the only one that can change them."

Don't place the blame anywhere but on your own shoulders. Once you take full ownership of all of the situations you have created, true change can begin.

You will, of course, need the assistance of other people on this life-changing journey. You may not succeed without the help of family, friends, business partners, coworkers, or anyone else that is a part of your life. It is possible to succeed without the help of others, but your journey to success will take much longer. The people that assist you will serve as your support group; they will be your team. Ask them for their opinion or advice when needed.

I believe we are all here to help one another in some form or fashion. So, don't be shy about asking for help when another opinion or perspective is needed. You may not like what they have to say, but it's probably something you need to hear.

But even with this team effort, you still have to be the leader, the quarterback of the team; you have to be the pilot, not the copilot, you have to be the driver of the car, not the passenger. Remember, your progression to success is, again, your ultimate responsibility. You will reap the benefits of success and learn the most from any setbacks or "perceived" failure.

Unfortunately, the word "failure" instills negative thoughts and attitudes. If at any time you feel you have failed at changing something, remember that you haven't failed. You simply learned how something was not supposed to be done. You can never "fail" if you learned something as a result of not accomplishing a task or goal.

Whenever you "fail" at something, you must, "Find an Interesting Lesson" in whatever you "failed" at doing.

With this, the lesson you learned from the "failure" will be applied to your next attempt until you succeed.

There isn't a sports athlete that makes every free throw, catches every pass, or wins every race. But with a minor adjustment here or there, they soon arrive in the winner's circle or hold the champion's trophy. It may even take years to find the right combination of choices, decisions, and actions before you succeed. But it has been proven time and time again that the repetition of the right combination of choices, decisions, and actions eventually leads to success.

When looking for what your real passion and value in life is because you want to be happy or have a void to fill, there are several questions you need to ask yourself.

Answering these questions carefully will allow you to better understand yourself and possibly discover what has hindered you from being happy and deepening your passions. Here are several questions you should ask yourself. You can take a notepad to answer these questions or memorize your answers. Writing your answers down on paper is generally recommended. You may also use these questions to help you start your MAP planner.

What interests you and really inspires you?

This may be difficult to answer, but you will certainly find the answer once you have answered the other questions. However, you need to be clear and specific about your source of inspiration. What is the kind of thing that you find exciting and that prompts you to take action?

. . .

If you were sure you would be successful, what would you do?

Many people do nothing because they are afraid of failing or have experienced failure in the past. If there was something you would do for sure if you knew there was no risk of failure, what would it be?

If you had to start all over again, what would you do?

A lot of people have put themselves in situations where they don't do what they want to do. They go to work because they have to but never experience the slightest pleasure in it. If you started all over again, would you take the opportunity to make a fresh start or would you take the same course again?

If money wasn't an issue, what would you do?

There are a lot of people who would like to chase their dreams but don't because they can't afford to get started. Think about what you would like to do if you had the cash. It could be anything.

What is your biggest dream?

What is your biggest dream, if you have one? There is

something you really want to do and dream of. Think about this thing and focus on it.

What is the biggest obstacle preventing you from following your dream?

List all the things that have kept you from achieving your biggest dreams so far. It could be people who don't support you, money, fears, or whatever. There are many obstacles of all types that can be overcome. You probably don't see the opportunities or success that come with your dreams, or you may be afraid of being laughed at by others. You may not have the ability or the talent. These are the kind of obstacles that may be holding you back.

What passion are you ashamed to admit?

Many people have dreams and passions they are afraid to reveal for fear of being laughed at by others. You may think that your passion will seem stupid to others. But what is this passion?

When you were a kid, who did you really want to be?

Did you dream of becoming someone when you were a kid, and did it turn out the way you had hoped? Do you still wonder what your life would be like today if you had pursued your childhood dreams? If you had the chance, would you follow your dream today?

If you were to die in the near future, what would you wish you hadn't done?

Many people have regrets when they realize they are about to die. It is then too late to go back and change the things they let slip. They would have lived their lives completely differently if they had had the chance. If a doctor told you that you only had a few weeks left to live, what would your regrets be? What would you like to do before you go?

Now that you've answered these questions, you should have a good idea of some of the things that make you happy, and some of your dreams. You need to have a clear idea of what it has always been your dream to do. Just think about what you would do with your money if you won the lotto. What would you do with yourself? Knowing these things is very important.

CHAPTER 9

FIND THE REAL YOU, THINK YOUR THOUGHTS

SELF-IMAGE, or your image, is the idea that everyone has of their own abilities, appearance, and personality. It is the mental picture that depicts not only the details objectively seen by others (such as height, weight, hair color, etc.), but also the elements that people have learned about themselves as a result of personal experiences and the insight of other people' opinions.

Self-image is nothing more than the result of the various images of how individuals see themselves, how they are seen by others, how they regard others, and how they regard themselves.

Self-image is a fundamental concept to understand because it is what determines our habits and approach to life.

In order to understand it in a simple way, we can define the image you have of yourself as the image you can see reflected in the mirror of your subconscious.

If the image of you present in your subconscious is

that of a failed and unhappy person, you will never be capable of acting inconsistently with the image you have of yourself, and therefore the subconscious, your autopilot, will lead you to perform all those actions that will give you timely confirmation of the unhappy and failed person you think you are.

A person who has an image of themselves as unhappy and a failure sees and regards themselves as such and believes that others see them as such and tends to have an inferiority complex toward others.

The image of your own self is not limited to a physical or personality representation of the person, but it defines the potential and abilities that that particular person can demonstrate in their life.

Let me give you an example of physical representation.

Have you ever seen a famous actress or a famous actor with a face practically deformed as a result of countless plastic surgery operations? Overblown cheekbones and lips, shiny skin that very often produces creepy results? Have you ever wondered why they did that to themselves?

The answer to this question lies in the image these people have of themselves. Self-image pushes them to carry out actions in a way that is commensurate with how a person pictures themselves.

People who see themselves as ugly or who do not accept the passage of time (always due to the fact that they do not see themselves as beautiful) tend to act in a manner consistent with the image they have of themselves, so that they are objectively uglier as time goes by. Their actions will tend to confirm the image they have of themselves. They go from one surgery to another because they are always dissatisfied with the result. Their problem is not physical but mental and therefore no surgery could solve it.

Everyone who behaves in this way needs more psychological help than a real change on a physical level.

Being able to understand the image of the ego is crucial to living a better life:

1. The image of the ego is the one that determines our actions, our behaviors, our feelings, our abilities, and therefore all our successes and failures.

2. The ego image can be changed at any time and there is no age limit to do so.

Do you understand the importance of this? If it is the image of the "I" that determines your actions, like a puppeteer who operates a puppet, you simply need to modify it to get a different life.

If you change the image you have of yourself, it will automatically and consistently change all your habits.

The self-image is like a sort of photograph or mental portrait of ourselves that is positioned in our subconscious.

. . .

Unfortunately, this image of ourselves is not clear and consciously difficult to determine, but we know it is there. When we try to think about it consciously, we can have the general idea of what kind of person we are and how we see ourselves, but we can't accurately determine all the details. Instead, the image of ourselves in our unconscious is very detailed: this is formed by all the concepts, thoughts, and information that are fixed in our subconscious. Since the subconscious accepts everything, it considers the image that has been formed within itself to be true, and consequently, cannot doubt it and makes the person act in a way that is consistent with the image itself on a daily basis.

But if it is possible to change the image of ourselves, why can't we change our lives despite often trying to change our habits?

The answer is simple: no effort to change our habits will be effective until we focus our attention on changing the image of ourselves which is what determines our habits.

You don't stop being afraid to speak in public by venturing into public because the consequent results would only validate your fears. The attention must be placed on changing the self-image initially, because this is what determines your habits.

It is your "I" that establishes the limitations that a person believes they have. The image you have of yourself is the one that decides whether you can successfully overcome a given situation. It does not matter if that limitation is easily within your reach or not.

They may have instilled in you the idea that you need to graduate in order to have a good career, but if the image you have of yourself is that of a person who does not want to study and who will not graduate, you will never get a degree. Yet, graduating is not an impassable limitation but a goal within everyone's reach. There are also those who manage to graduate by studying less than necessary because they have a confident image of themselves during exams. Those who are terrified of appearing before a professor despite having studied a lot are systematically panicked.

If your ego represents a fat person, you will never be able to change your physical appearance because, despite the daily effort to change your habits, your autopilot will always take you back to acting in a way that satisfies the image you have of yourself. Getting up from your seat to go for a run will always be an enormous effort, and it will always be in vain because, when you are on autopilot, you will open the refrigerator and eat until all your efforts are wasted. On the contrary, by replacing the old fat image with a slimmer one, you will start to act with more determination, with less effort, and above all in a way consistent with your new self. Your autopilot will no longer guide you to the fridge!

Anyone can be thin, but only those who see themselves as thin are thin in reality. Those who see themselves as fat have an image of the ego that places an impassable limitation of weight, a limitation below which the person is convinced that they cannot go lower.

It is precisely for this reason that a person who has to

lose weight is often advised to set themselves small goals, so that they can be easily reached and so that every small success pushes them with greater conviction towards the next goal. You are doing nothing but trying to change the limitations imposed by your ego, proving from time to time that they are only mental limitations. The truth is that if you are in this situation, the easiest way is to change the image you have of yourself, and you will see that everything will be more natural, and you will automatically act according to your new self.

But right now, I tell you more to show you the power of the image you have of yourself fixed in your subconscious: it is not necessarily fat people who have a fat image of themselves.

Does the phrase "that girl behaves like that because she sees herself as being fat but doesn't want to accept it" come to mind? And yet she is a girl in perfect physical shape!

Among the various factors that determine anorexia nervosa, characterized by fear of gaining weight and an altered perception of weight, there are temperamental and environmental factors, both of which can be traced back to experiences during childhood, where, for example, you lived in an environment where slimness was considered a value.

In order to resolve these cases, we do not intervene exclusively with medical-nutritional figures; the support of psychiatric figures is crucial to act on the patient's mind.

Those who have a fat self-image, regardless of

whether they are fat or thin in reality, will also have a problem with their perception of weight. It is the same principle previously observed in those who exaggerate with plastic surgery.

As you can see, all the information you are acquiring is related to each other. The possibility of having an overview will be crucial for you to be able to change the image of yourself.

There are people everywhere around us who are constantly getting hurt, people who are constantly repeating huge mistakes, people who are always acting in the same way. They talk, discuss, make plans, make promises, but then they always start complaining and behaving according to the image they have of themselves.

RID YOURSELF OF LIMITING BELIEFS

You've done it, you've defeated the saboteur. You've accomplished something that most people never even attempt and fewer still succeed at. You have silenced the little voice in your head that tries to hold you back and keep you from reaching your goals and dreams. Even more impressive is the fact that you not only defeated the saboteur, you replaced its influence with a positive and reaffirming voice.

CHAPTER 10

REPROGRAMMING YOUR HABITS

YOU SHOULD BE proud of what you have accomplished, but you shouldn't be satisfied. This was simply another step on the path to long-term success. It was an important step, but you need to remain hungry and remember that your journey is far from over.

The moment that you stop striving to improve and move forward is the moment when you will start to lose your ability to reach your goals and dreams. You have already accomplished so much, so don't make the mistake of allowing this hard work to be in vain. Continue the journey, continue to work hard, and you can accomplish anything you set your mind to.

While the saboteur may have been vanquished, there's still a good chance that you retain some of the limiting beliefs that once fueled it's surprisingly potent voice. Limiting beliefs are the beliefs that you have that occupy your subconscious mind and influence you in a negative way. They try to get you to give up on the hopes and dreams that you have and instead accept a more normal path in life.

While limiting beliefs are a part of your core personality, they are not usually the result of your own mind's actions. Instead, they are the accumulated influence of the people around you who have told you that you cannot reach your unrealistic dreams. While the saboteur cannot exist without limiting beliefs, limiting beliefs can still linger within you even after you have defeated the influence of the saboteur.

What is it that you truly want out of life? What is it that is important to you and drives you to continue on a path toward self-improvement? Is it acquiring great wealth? Is it starting a successful business? How about having great health? What you need to remember is that these are all goals that you can reach. The only thing that can hold you back from getting what you want is your own lack of action and ambition. Will you encounter obstacles in your path that can become major setbacks? Of course, life is full of unforeseen problems that can derail your plans. But it's up to you if the problems will prove to be too much to overcome.

While some things can prove to be truly catastrophic in the effect that they have upon us, they don't have to mean the end of your ambitions.

Instead of allowing limiting beliefs to fester in the recesses of your subconscious mind, you need to exorcise them. You need to expel them from your core beliefs and replace them with the positive energy of reaffirming thoughts.

Limiting beliefs live in your subconscious, and you probably aren't even aware of their negative influence most of the time. Even though you don't recognize that they are there, their influence can be significant. They can create a conflict with your conscious mind that results in you becoming indecisive and unwilling to take necessary risks. You may not realize it, but having any type of limiting beliefs can be very disruptive to you and what you want to accomplish. The conflict between your subconscious and conscious thoughts can sap you of the energy and will that you need in order to continue striving to reach your hopes and dreams.

Instead of allowing limiting beliefs to take up valuable space in your mind and draw upon the energy you need to make positive progress, you need to expel them. You need to do more than this, however; you need to replace them. You need positive thoughts to occupy the space that was once reserved for housing your limiting beliefs.

How do you accomplish this? You do it by refusing to accept that self-doubt has a place in your heart. You silence the self-doubt that plagues most people by telling yourself that you can do anything you want, and that nothing is beyond your ability. Most people can't do this. Most people are unable to change their mindset, but you don't have to be like most people. Over time, as you continue to purge limiting beliefs from your mind, they will inevitably be replaced with positive thoughts and energy. The vacuum that is created when negativity is eliminated must be filled with a much more useful type of positive energy.

If you want to truly have a chance at reaching the goals and dreams that you have, then you must have absolute belief in your ability to do so. You must know deep down in your core that if you can conceive of something, then you can achieve it. Only when you are able to do this will you truly have the capacity to accomplish great things.

When you don't have this ability, when your core personality is not aligned in such a way that you know that you can do it, then you will be doomed to failure. If your core personality isn't purged of all limiting beliefs, then they will multiply and overtake you. Much like a cancer will intrude upon your body, limiting beliefs will fill your mind and sap your ability to realize your true potential.

Will it be easy to rid yourself of limiting beliefs and replace them with positive thoughts and energy? Much like everything else that you must do to reach your goals and dreams, it will be a challenge. But it is a challenge you must accept.

Do you want to conform to the rules and expectations of society? Do you want to accept that you will never be truly happy because you will never realize your hopes and dreams? Or do you want to strive for something greater than most people would ever dare to? If you can purge limiting beliefs from your subconscious, then you can build a mindset that allows you to accomplish anything you can imagine.

You should understand how important it is to have a growth mentality and a positive image of your "I," as these are all that determine the successes and failures that a person achieves in their life.

Do you still want to wait and burn off what little time you have left standing behind all the nonvirtuous thoughts you unfortunately have fixed in your subconscious?

When you are young, you believe that time never passes, but the truth is that it runs inexorably, and what we have at our disposal is nothing more than a breath of life.

Every opportunity lost in the street is a missed opportunity. At this point in the book, you should feel the desire to change, the desire to detach yourself from your old habits and change your future for the better.

Although many of these concepts are abstract, you have been able to see how they are demonstrated in real life, and you have probably also seen yourself reflected in some examples that I have used to better define the information I have presented to you. If you really want to change for the better, don't waste any more time; make sure you have no regrets in the future.

Reprogramming your mind is possible, but it is a path that will put you to the test, especially in the first few days or weeks, because it will take some time before you start to notice changes.

Moreover, the path to follow will not be the same for everyone, not only because the desires change from person to person and therefore the bad habits to change are also different, but also because everyone lives in a different context. Living in a depowering environment does not preclude the possibility of being able to change your mindset for the better, but it will certainly take more time and much more determination.

So, before talking about the various exercises that will help you reprogram your mind, it is necessary to start by changing the surrounding environment and daily routine as much as possible.

The best solution to be able to reprogram your mind in the best way and in the shortest possible time is twofold:

- isolation
- total immersion

Isolating yourself from the world, from negative people (which doesn't mean bad!), from the wrong daily routine, from the pessimistic information coming from television or newspapers, from the temptations you may encounter around every corner. is definitely the first point to start from. This is the way to completely immerse yourself in this new path of change and regeneration.

Of course, I understand that there are few people who can adopt such a solution. Most of those who will read this book, especially those who are no longer young, probably have many commitments to carry on (with work or family) and cannot afford to go into total immersion by isolating themselves from the world.

In this case, even if with more difficulty and the need for greater determination, it is still possible to achieve the desired result. However, the important thing is to reduce to a minimum the negative impacts that you have with your daily routine.

For example, you could use these measures:

Laziness and determination

The first point on the list can be nothing other than laziness. Basically, you are a lazy being. We are all lazy beings. Some are lazier, some less so, but all human beings are basically lazy. Perhaps even while reading this book you had a few moments of weakness that led you to temporarily lose focus.

A weakness can be of any kind, like addiction to social networks, mobile phones, TV, lying on the couch, sex, smoking... and so on. These and other similar habits make you lose focus. While you are reading, a notification appears on your smartphone. What do you do? You have to identify the habits that make you distract yourself, avoid indulging in them, and replace them. You need to be determined in what you do!

If you commit yourself today to adopting virtuous habits while others are busy having fun while satisfying their bad habits, one day you will be able to enjoy everything you want, and they will only dream about it.

Television

Try to turn off the television for good. Avoid watching news and programs that talk about problems or talk shows that are swarming with people who have uncertainties, doubts, difficulties, and problems in general. No more watching programs where people are crying and despairing. If you really have to watch TV, documentaries or comedy films will be preferable. Laughter is always good, whatever the circumstances. In case there are serious problems (for instance, there is the COVID-19 problem at the moment of writing), you have to limit yourself to getting to know what is strictly useful and necessary for you and forgetting all the talk shows and debates connected to them. Take note of it, archive it, and return to focusing on your goal.

Newspapers and magazines

The same applies to newspapers as to television. Avoid both newspapers and gossip magazines. If you really want to have fun, opt for a crossword puzzle.

Internet and social networks

Use the internet intelligently and exclusively to inform yourself about what you really need to achieve your goal. Avoid social networks like a plague and never get dragged into pointless discussions that won't change anything for you. Avoid reading the comments of people who are now hopeless and use the internet as an outlet for all their frustrations. Remember that if something won't change your life in a positive way, then it won't do you any good. Don't waste any more time. Make it a habit to ask yourself, every time you do something or write something, will what I am doing help me in any way to achieve my goal? You will see that you will often back out of useless discussions.

Politics

Unless you are a politician or want to become a politician, don't get involved in politics. Politics only leads to discussions centered on problems that everyone has and that no one can solve simply by chatting. Politics leads to discussions about personal problems, economic problems, problems at work, and corruption. Leave politics to politicians. Don't expect political discussions to help you or even the politicians themselves. By this point in the book, you should have realized that only you can help yourself. Focus on yourself and assume your responsibilities. No politician or political party will solve your problems. If you are in a difficult situation, it is not the fault of others, be they partners, business owners, friends, or politicians. You can change your life! Only you can!

Smartphones

Delete all unnecessary WhatsApp groups (for example, if you have young children, you cannot delete a group with school communications even though it is full of parents who complain about everything. Always avoid unnecessary discussions and limit them to what is strictly necessary). Make sure you don't have hundreds of notifications every day that distract you from your real goal, then deactivate the Facebook notifications, the games notifications, and all of those that are not absolutely necessary.

Friends

Changing your behavior with friends and family, whether at home, at work, or during school time, will not be easy. But you know full well that the subconscious accepts everything—it does not distinguish right from wrong, reality from imagination. You cannot continue to hang out with people who throw negative ideas at you because, even if you consciously wish not to listen to them, your subconscious hears them, and, if they are appropriate to your paradigms, it accepts them without hesitation.

Do you really think you can change your nonvirtuous habits by continuing to live as you have done so far and with the same external stimuli? Do you really want to continue spending time with friends, talking about economic problems or problems at work?

Even if you think it's hard to stay away from your friends for a long time, this is something you must absolutely do. People with a growth mentality cannot be joined by people with a negative mindset. Do you know any of them? People with the same mindset seek and find each other because they travel on the same frequency. People with a negative mindset come together in groups and tend to dump their problems on each other. I will reiterate once again that they are not bad people, but their behavior is certainly not helpful to those who want to change their lives.

I am also anticipating something that will happen in your near future and that you will now find hard to believe: once you succeed in reprogramming your mind by substituting old nonvirtuous habits with new virtuous habits, you will no longer have the desire to meet old acquaintances. You will only desire to meet people who have the same mentality as you.

You will change friends, you will change acquaintances, you will automatically become a new person.

Now you will find it hard to believe it, but I can assure you that this will be the case, and you will never have any second thoughts.

Job

At the workplace, you will have to avoid discussions and complaints and only carry out the tasks that are required of you. Don't get dragged into the usual discussions about strikes, wage increases, payroll, holidays, etc. Also, try to avoid spending lunch breaks with your colleagues and take advantage of them by doing mental reprogramming exercises.

. . .

Family life

While you can detach yourself from your friends for a period of time without many problems, the situation is very different in the family. If you are married, the first advice I want to give you is to talk to your partner. This is for two basic reasons. First of all, doing this mental reprogramming as a couple is very advantageous. The second reason is that your partner needs to be made aware that you are going to change your daily routine, and you need to feel their support. After a few days of immersion, you will inevitably start to change, not wanting to face the usual everyday conversations at the table, often focused on topics about the scarcity of money (the bills, the holiday you can't take which is too expensive to afford, yet another invitation to a wedding, etc.). This point is fundamental because what will happen with your friends (from whom you will inevitably distance yourself due to "lack of feeling") could really cast doubt on the family union. There is nothing to be ashamed of—talk to your partner and express your desire to improve, let them understand how the whole family life could improve. Ask your partner to read this book as well and avoid having unnecessary discussions. They should simply take note of your effort and should not obstruct you in any way.

On the other hand, if you are a person living at home with your parents, you have to acknowledge that although they are the people who love you the most on this Earth, they are human like everyone else and, like most people, have the wrong paradigms. If your paradigms are not correct, the paradigms of those who raised you will certainly not be correct. Try to isolate yourself as much as possible and avoid any discussions. Take everything that is good from them and let everything that can affect your path of change leave your mind. If you have the financial capacity to rent a house, do it and take the opportunity to complete a full immersion for as long as necessary.

I think you now understand how you need to radically change your approach to everyday life in order to reprogram your mind. Initially, it will be a difficult path with many obstacles and temptations. However, as the days go by, you will realize that not only will many things become easier for you, but that you will even start to act automatically in certain different circumstances. You'll immediately recognize powerless discourses and walk away from them, you'll no longer engage in unproductive controversy, and you'll also begin to see successful people from a different point of view.

Reprogramming your mind means reprogramming your habits. This does not mean eliminating bad habits, but it means replacing bad habits with healthy habits. Emptiness does not exist! If you don't change a habit from bad to virtuous, you risk creating an unhealthy habit.

CONCLUSION

Congratulations! You have almost reached the end of this book. I truly hope you have enjoyed the experience of reading it and have gained a lot of value from it, because I have gained much from writing it. Writing helps to gather and organize all of the thoughts from your head and helps you look at the material from another perspective. As they say, you'll learn a lot more about a subject by teaching it.

Keeping a journal will help you to remember the important things, just writing ideas down on paper by hand has wonderful properties; it will give you a better memory of these ideas, better comprehension, and a better perspective than typing it down on your mobile phone or a computer. Writing ideas and goals down on paper is also the first step of manifestation.

Let's summarize what we've learned about the power of belief, identifying and overcoming limiting beliefs, and the valuable strategies that will help you not only maintain your newly found fundamental beliefs but also succeed in your life and career.

Belief is the conviction that something is true. However, most beliefs are formed in the absence of evidence. It's important to remember that beliefs are not a guide to the truth. The purpose of belief is to guide action, not to indicate truth. This is why one person is able to believe in their goals and take action to achieve them, while others are overwhelmed by self-doubt and have no power to press forward.

Your reality is created by your beliefs, so consequently you are creating your own luck, happiness, and everything else. Your brain matches the information it receives to the beliefs you have. What doesn't fit is simply discarded. This is why it's important to adopt and maintain fundamental empowering beliefs.

Our beliefs are formed from an early age. Most beliefs are formed during childhood. Unfortunately, not all of us have had great supportive parents and teachers. As a result, most of us have formed various limiting beliefs during our formative years. These limiting beliefs can greatly inhibit our abilities during adult life.

However, if we adopted those limiting beliefs, it means we can adopt new fundamental beliefs to replace them. First, you need to establish which beliefs you have in general. You can do that by writing down all of your beliefs.

Then, you have to establish which beliefs are limiting you and which ones are helpful, so you can keep them. When examining your beliefs, keep in mind how useful a belief is in your particular situation in relation to the goals that you are trying to achieve. If it assists and supports you in reaching those goals, then keep it. But if it doesn't help and hinders your progress, this is obviously a clear sign that you are dealing with a limiting belief.

At this point, it's important to remember your beliefs are not the truth. Remember that your limiting beliefs are assumptions you make about reality that are not necessarily true.

To overcome your limiting beliefs, first make a list of beliefs that have held you back. Now, take one of your beliefs and think of a time when it wasn't true. Examine how this belief has held you back. Try to remember when you first adopted this belief. Now, think of the benefits you gained from limiting beliefs. Sometimes limiting beliefs can have a purpose.

Finally, visualize getting rid of this belief. Imagine it as a wooden tablet that you throw far into the ocean with immense force, and it disappears over the horizon. Now, think of a statement opposite to that belief, write it down, and say it out loud. This is your new fundamental empowering belief. Now, repeat this process for all your limiting beliefs.

Your newly found fundamental beliefs have to be maintained. As a quick fix, if you find yourself dwelling on negative thoughts, try to shift your negative self-talk into the past tense. For sustaining them long term, there are certain techniques that we will reiterate now.

The first step to building self-confidence is facing your fears. It's important to keep in mind that if something feels scary, it doesn't necessarily mean that it's risky. You can overcome your fears by educating yourself on what risks are actually involved when doing things that scare you. Then you can create an action plan on how to approach overcoming your fears step by step. Another thing you can do is challenge your thoughts that don't necessarily make sense. Facing your fears is a great way to reduce anxiety and build more self-confidence.

Get moving to calm your body and mind. This will help you relax and release the tension. Introduce some mindful rhythmic movement routines into your daily life. It can be anything: walking, jogging, gardening, Hatha Yoga, or swimming. Considering that anxiety is the result of feeling stuck in our thoughts. being unable to resolve something. Rhythmic movement will help you get out of your head. Rhythmic movement improves your mood, reduces emotional stress and inflammation, and enhances your immune system. It makes you more relaxed and focused and increases your feeling of security. It's exactly what we need in our daily struggles.

Next are the big three: mindfulness, responsibility, and acceptance.

If our minds are left undirected, they can make us anxious and unhappy in many different ways. Mindfulness provides the ability to feel happy and content in any circumstances, despite any worries you might have. It also helps find a connection to something beyond our concerns. It brings an increased awareness of our connection to others and our surroundings, which in turn provides a deeper understanding of your life, thus making us content. Another huge benefit of practicing mindfulness is the ability to cultivate the observing self. It will help you see yourself separately from your ego and personality, which in turn will allow you to see what areas need improvement. It will help you detach from your thoughts and emotions and see things more clearly.

Responsibility is the ability to determine your response to any circumstances. It is the ultimate habit of a person who possesses high personal effectiveness. It gives you the feeling of real freedom that nobody and nothing can take away. Responsibility allows you to make the most important decision—to be proactive over your responses. It will help you learn how to approach any problems you might face and where to focus your time and energy.

Acceptance is the process of experiencing your feelings directly, without filtering or sorting them. Acceptance is the willingness and ability to experience yourself and your life as is. Acceptance should flow from mindfulness practice, as it helps you lose your identification with your thoughts and establish what you might not be accepting. Acceptance helps you be content with anything you can't change. It allows you to move from self-deception towards reality.

Remember, your environment can subconsciously influence you in many forms. We always hear how the environment we grew up in shaped us into who we are today. The same principle applies now, in the present. If you feel stuck, you should consider changing your mental and physical environment. Change your social circle.

End your toxic relationships and friendships. See how you can change your physical environment on the micro level. Change up your living space. If you can, consider the possibility of moving altogether. You need to change in order to grow, and changing your environment is a transformative experience. If you change your environment for the better, you will see positive changes in your life.

Our daily lives are full of discomfort. But the key to success is in the things we tend to avoid. When you encounter any challenges, you have to become more than you were in order to overcome them. Naturally, this may cause a fair share of discomfort. Learning to accept discomfort and being comfortable with it is one of the most valuable skills you can possess. If you learn to accept discomfort, you can master pretty much anything.

Now that we've learned the techniques and strategies to improve our daily life and maintain fundamental beliefs, let's focus on the long-term goals. Adopting a long-term thinking mindset is crucial to succeed in your life and career. Long-term thinking allows you to focus on your larger long-term goals instead of getting stuck in the moment and obsessing over setbacks. Furthermore, it will help you make the things you enjoy in the short term match up with your long-term goals. The main idea of the long-term thinking mindset is that there is always an action, no matter how small, that you can take that will bring you closer to your bigger long-term goals.

Finally, developing your emotional intelligence will help you master your emotions and use them to your advantage. Developing emotional intelligence can improve your understanding of yourself and others. It can help raise your awareness of your circumstances and improve your ability to act in your own best interests and the best interests of people around you.

Constant self-improvement is the key to success. Remember to examine your beliefs from time to time. You may find you've adopted some new limiting or negative beliefs, and that's okay. You can always take the necessary steps to replace them with empowering beliefs.

Don't forget that your new fundamental beliefs need maintenance. React in the moment by shifting your negative self-talk into the past tense.

Use mindfulness to take a look at yourself from the point of view of an observer. Determine which areas of your life need improvement and work on them.

Introduce a mindful rhythmic movement routine into your daily life to release the accumulated tension, calm your body and mind and keep staying relaxed.

Focus on the long-term goals with the power of long-term thinking. Don't allow temporary setbacks to throw you off course.

Any time you feel demotivated, come and read this book again. We tend to neglect and forget the most useful and important instruments we possess. This book contains all the tools you need to overcome self-doubt, boost your self-confidence, and succeed in your life and career.

By now you have a range of ideas on how you can start taking some steps to improve your life. There is no right or wrong way of doing this, as long as there is some sort of improvement to the choices you make. You can do it any way you like—you can do things that I did or do it some other way. It doesn't matter, everyone's circumstances are different, and what worked for me might not work for you. I also would like you to find as many mentors as you possibly can, to get perspective. But if you choose to follow my steps, I will quickly recap the most important points of this book.

Start with baby steps. Begin investing your time in your education, a lot of time. I know that you might think that you're already smart, and you don't need to read books. You also might be looking for get-rich-quick strategies, but there is no such thing, I'm sorry. Investing in your education is a lifelong process and should never end. It is the cheapest and safest investment strategy, with a very large return on investment and practically nonexistent disadvantages. Read and listen to as many books as you possibly can and listen to each book 6-10 times. It will soon become the most valuable habit you can have, a habit of accumulating knowledge.

Start paying attention to what kind of food you are putting in your body. If you are completely honest and can admit to yourself that your eating habits aren't the healthiest, and you can't say that you feel good or great daily, but rather you feel "normal," you probably are not feeling very well, and you have felt like crap for so long that feeling like crap is a normal for you. That's how I felt for the longest time, until I changed. You will not be able to feel the difference unless you change your diet for something much healthier. When I started eating mostly vegetables, fish, and chicken, cut off white sugar, and limited all sorts of breads to a minimum, I can tell you that the way I feel today is amazing. I haven't been sick for years, I have tons of energy, I feel a lot happier, and I feel even happier when I look in the mirror!

Combining a healthy diet, regular exercise, meditation, 7-8 hours of sleep, and doing it consistently will transform your life forever.

Start paying attention to what you let in your mind. If you want to feel the difference, take a break from the usual media and also take a break from everything negative for one week. Stop watching mainstream news and everything related to action, violence, war, drama, horror, etc. And instead watch nonviolent media, like comedies, nature documentaries, funny videos on YouTube, etc. I know what you are thinking, this is boring as hell, and I agree! But try it for a week and you will be surprised. You will become a more positive and happier person even by just doing this.

Stop saving money for the sake of saving money. Instead, save money to buy or create assets that produce passive income. Buy assets such as rental real estate or paper assets like stocks, bonds, mutual funds, IPOs etc., or create assets such as businesses and use businesses to buy other assets. In fact, ebooks and ecommerce businesses are also a form of an asset that will produce passive income through royalties. I'm not a financial expert, so you should make sure to talk to a qualified financial expert and do a lot of study and research about the subject before investing.

Make a commitment for change, promise this for yourself. Make this the day that you will decide to change. It is a long and difficult road to success, it is hard work, you are going to want to quit many times, you will fail, but you will also get back up and continue. You will learn from your failures and you will also win.

Yes, the path to success in anything is difficult, but so is normal life. So, if both are difficult, why not choose the path where there is an unlimited upside, rather than the path for mediocrity?

So, if you ask, what will the next few years bring? If you don't change, the next few years are going to be pretty much the same as they always have been.

Make this choice to change not only for yourself, but also for your family, your loved ones, and everyone else as well, so you can be an example for them for what a person can become and what greatness can be achieved.

REFERENCES

References

A list of 12 values and beliefs to guide your life. (2011, July 24). Mazzastick. https://www.mazzastick.com/12-values-and-beliefs-to-guide-your-life

Ackerman, C. E. (2018, December 22). *What is self-image and how do we improve it? Definition + quotes.* PositivePsychology.com. https://positivepsychology.com/self-image

Belief. (n.d.). Encyclopedia Britannica. Retrieved July 30, 2020, from https://www.britannica.com/topic/belief

Buckley, L. (2019, June 6). *The differences between your conscious and subconscious mind.* Marisa Peer. https://marisapeer.com/the-differences-between-your-conscious-and-subconscious-mind/

Chalmers, D. J. (1996). *The conscious mind: in search of a theory of conscious experience.* Oxford University Press.

Clover, A. (2012, October 9). *Why your subconscious*

keeps you from greatness (& what to do about it). Possibility Change. https://possibilitychange.com/subconscious-saboteurs

Demers, D. (n.d.). *How to reprogram your mind*. Beliefnet. https://www.beliefnet.com/wellness/articles/how-to-reprogram-your-mind.aspx

Fairytale, E. (n.d.). *Candles and incense for meditation*. https://www.pexels.com/photo/candles-and-incense-for-meditation-3822622/

Fernyhough, C. (2010, August 16). *What do we mean by "thinking"?* Psychology Today. https://www.psychologytoday.com/us/blog/the-voices-within/201008/what-do-we-mean-thinking

Ho, L. (2020, March 9). *How to change habits by using your subconscious mind*. Lifehack. https://www.lifehack.org/865931/change-habits

How to set personal development goals for work (with examples). (2020, November 24). Indeed. https://www.indeed.com/career-advice/career-development/personal-development-goals-for-work

iMotions. (2019, February 18). *What is the subconscious mind? - A scientific explanation*. IMotions. https://imotions.com/blog/what-is-the-subconscious-mind/

Inner critic. (2015, October 8). GoodTherapy.org. https://www.goodtherapy.org/blog/psychpedia/inner-critic#:~:text=Inner%20critic%20refers%20to%20an

Lewis, R. (2018). *What actually is a belief? And why is it so hard to change?* Psychology Today. https://www.psychologytoday.com/us/blog/finding-purpose/201810/what-actually-is-belief-and-why-is-it-so-hard-change

Lewis, R. (2019, February 24). *What actually is a thought? And how is information physical?* Psychology Today. https://www.psychologytoday.com/us/blog/finding-purpose/201902/what-actually-is-thought-and-how-is-information-physical

Magic Bowls. (n.d.). *Tibetan singing bowls.* https://www.pexels.com/photo/tibetan-singing-bowls-3543912/

Malu, B. (n.d.). *Photo of a sign and eyeglasses on table.* https://www.pexels.com/photo/photo-of-a-sign-and-eyeglasses-on-table-1485657/

Mcafee, D. G., & Harrison, C. (2018). *The belief book.* Atheist Republic.

Migaj, S. (n.d.). *Person on a bridge near a lake.* https://www.pexels.com/photo/person-on-a-bridge-near-a-lake-747964/

Mindfulness. (n.d.). Psychology Today. https://www.psychologytoday.com/intl/basics/mindfulness

Riopel, L. (2020, September 1). *21 self-image examples and activities to use the theory today.* https://positivepsychology.com/self-image-examples-activities

Schwandt, J. (2018, February 16). *How to reprogram your brain like a computer and hack your habits.* Lifehack. https://www.lifehack.org/673096/how-to-hack-your-brain-and-reprogram-your-habits-like-a-computer

Snapwire. (n.d.). *Silhouette of man raising his hands.*

https://www.pexels.com/photo/achievement-confident-free-freedom-6945/

Staff, SUCCESS. (2017, August 24). *Jim Rohn on working harder on yourself than your job*. SUCCESS. www.success.com/jim-rohn-on-working-harder-on-your-self-than-your-job/

Tracy, B. (2018, December 12). *The power of your subconscious mind*. Brian Tracy. https://www.briantracy.com/blog/personal-success/understanding-your-subconscious-mind/

Tony, T. (2017, February 9). *6 strategic tips to reprogram your mind*. Tony Robbins. https://www.tonyrobbins.com/mind-meaning/how-to-reprogram-your-mind/

Printed in Great Britain
by Amazon

20394821R00088